SELECTED PROSE AND POETRY
OF JULES SUPERVIELLE

Edited, with an Introduction by Nancy Kline

Prose translated by Nancy Kline

Poetry translated by

Patricia Terry & Kathleen Micklow

BLACK
WIDOW
PRESS

Street view of Paris at dusk.

SELECTED PROSE AND POETRY OF JULES SUPERVIELLE

Edited, with an Introduction by Nancy Kline

Prose translated by Nancy Kline

Poetry translated by

Patricia Terry & Kathleen Micklow

Black Widow Press is an imprint of Commonwealth Books, Inc., Boston, MA. Distributed to the trade by NBN (National Book Network) throughout North America, Canada, and the U.K. All Black Widow Press books are printed on acid-free paper, and glued into bindings. Black Widow Press and its logo are registered trademarks of Commonwealth Books, Inc.

Joseph S. Phillips and Susan J. Wood, Ph.D., Publishers
www.blackwidowpress.com

Cover photo: Jules Supervielle ©Martinie/Roger-Viollet / The Image Works
Production: Kerrie Kemperman

ISBN-13: 978-0-9856122-3-8

Printed in the United States

10 9 8 7 6 5 4 3 2 1

for Pat

ACKNOWLEDGMENTS

Our deepest thanks to Jean-Pierre Bourgeois who braved the *bouquinistes* along the Seine and came home with a precious crumbling copy of *L'Arche de Noé,* long since out of print; to the Virginia Center for the Creative Arts, whose vibrant silence and cows and artists helped to foster this translation; to Rebecca Guy, Anne-Marie Mairesse, Michael Carman, Victoria Hallerman, Polly Howells, and Susan Sindall, and Evelyn Barish, Betty Boyd Caroli, Carol Hebald, and Dorothy O. Helly for their insightful readings; to Jacqueline Lhoumeau for her invaluable help on this project, as on so many others; to Kerrie Kemperman for her patient excellence in editing; and to Joe Phillips who still loves books made of ink and paper and brings them into being.

TABLE OF CONTENTS

INTRODUCTION

From his apartment in Paris, the poet reaches up into outer space to hang his parents' portraits between two trembling stars; he carves a mantelpiece below them out of "hard night" ("47 Boulevard Lannes"). Elsewhere, he conducts us to the sheared-off main street of a tiny French town, floating in the middle of the ocean. The little girl who lives there in utter solitude, forever, is dead ("Child of the High Seas"). In his forests, star-crossed lovers kill themselves to be reborn as living birches, entirely indifferent now to those they've left behind, who grieve for them ("The Little Wood"); beneath the sea, the drowned continue to exist in colonies of Streaming Creatures, cut off from the living but still behaving as the living do ("The Unknown Girl of the Seine"); and when the poet turns his eyes on his own body, it is to search among his fingernails for a fingernail belonging to his long-dead mother or to seek one of her lashes mixed in with his own ("The Portrait").

The critic Marcel Raymond has called Jules Supervielle "the poet of metempsychoses, of metamorphoses,…of mysterious telepathies, thanks to which…all things communicate invisibly, exchanging their fluids and their messages."[i] In like manner, Étiemble speaks of the poet's "obsession with… osmosis between the dead and the living."[ii] And indeed, in Supervielle's dizzyingly fluid poetic universe—where boundaries blur between earth and sky, sea and land, nymphs and trees—the membrane that connects and separates the living and the dead is permeable, but not entirely; often to their mutual sorrow. All human yearnings to the contrary, we lose our dead, as we are lost to them, and what remains between us is our absence from each other. In this poetic universe, even God is isolated, "cut off from [his] creation" and from himself ("God's Sorrow").

Despite which, to read Supervielle's stories and poems is exhilirating, spun out as they are in his distinctive voice: rueful, funny, forthright, tender, sometimes bitingly satiric, by turns lyrical and abrupt.

★

The 20th-century French poet Jules Supervielle was born in Montevideo, Uruguay, in 1884. His young French parents had moved there to participate in the founding of a family bank. When he was eight months old, the couple took their baby back to France to visit relatives in Basque country. There, within a week of each other, both his parents died, poisoned by tainted water they had unwittingly drunk.

The baby remained in France with his grandmother until he was two, at which time he returned to Uruguay to live out what was, by his account, a happy childhood (see "The Estancia"). The boy grew up believing that his aunt and uncle were his biological parents and his cousins his siblings. Until one day a friend of his aunt's blithely inquired, in Supervielle's nine-year-old presence: *Is he your sister's child, Marie-Anne? This little one?* This was the first time Supervielle had ever heard of his dead parents, whose actual portraits he was not shown until several years later.[iii]

At the age of ten, the boy left Montevideo for Paris, to study at the Lycée Janson de Sailly. Many summers, he sailed back across the Atlantic, spending long school vacations in Uruguay, which confirmed his sense of being rooted in two countries—and in neither altogether, part of him "always elsewhere"[iv]—in two cultures and languages, separated and conjoined by the immensity of the sea. All of this found its way into his work, which he began to publish in 1900: his earliest poems, *Brumes du passé (Mists of the Past),* appeared that year. He earned his baccalaureat in 1902, did his military service in 1903–4, then earned his *licence ès lettres* at the Sorbonne, in Spanish language and literature, in 1906.

For the rest of his life, Supervielle would live and write in Paris, an older and more self-conscious society than Uruguay, to which he equally belonged. But everything he wrote—and he wrote prolifically: poems, tales, memoirs, novels, plays—was marked, if not explicitly, by the violence, the untamed beauty and untenanted spaciousness of the Uruguayan pampas, flat vast mirrors to the Atlantic Ocean.[v] It was in Uruguay that the poet met and married his wife, Pilar Saavedra. There they had the first of their six children and later spent the long years of the Second World War (1939–1946).

This French poet's experience of Uruguay was further reinforced by his reading of two earlier and quite extraordinary nineteenth-century French poets, Lautréamont (1846–1870) and Laforgue (1860–1887), whom Supervielle claimed as his predecessors. Both, like him, were born in

Montevideo of French parents; both returned to live and work in France. Supervielle's "Child of the High Seas" seems a direct descendant of the heroine of Laforgue's tale "Perseus and Andromeda."[vi] And in "To Lautréamont" the ancestor-poet makes his way directly onto Supervielle's page. Here, the speaker of the poem goes looking for Lautréamont, long since dead. The earlier poet repeatedly refuses to appear, until

> On the very day of my death I see you coming toward me
> With your human face.
> You stroll encouragingly, barefoot among the lofty clumps of
> the sky,
> But when you are just close enough
> You hurl one in my face,
> Lautréamont.

This violent, surprising, irreverent gesture of recognition seems entirely in keeping with Supervielle's portrait, in another text, of the Uruguayan gaucho who greets a long-lost friend by playfully engaging him in a knife fight ("Gauchos").

The French Surrealists also claimed Lautréamont for their own, which makes it all the more striking that their contemporary, Supervielle, was never associated with Surrealism. He was not particularly interested in its doctrines and procedures, in free association or the unconscious. Nevertheless he knew and was known to them and to other twentieth-century writers, among whom he had good friends, including Henri Michaux, Rainer Maria Rilke, Jean Paulhan, and René Étiemble.

At the time of his death in Paris, in 1960, Supervielle was possessed of two titles, the first awarded him by Uruguay: Honorary Cultural Attaché at the Uruguayan Embassy to France, and the second by France itself: Prince of Poets.

★

The present anthology of his work is as quirky as its author and his translators. In his time, Supervielle was above all celebrated for his poetry. But we agree with Étiemble, who remarks that often "Supervielle is more a poet in his tales than in his verses,"[vii] and our anthology leans toward his prose, containing two chapters from the memoir *Uruguay* and ten tales, along with seventeen of his major poems. All poems appear bilingually, in French and English; prose appears only in English.

We have not separated poetry and prose into generic baskets in the following pages. Rather, we have intermingled genres—as the poet did, over the course of his long life, alternating between verse and prose, sometimes taking poems and transforming them into tales (*e.g.,* "Child of the High Seas," "The Little Wood"). Nor have we arranged his texts in order of their publication, but rather in echo to each other, juxtaposing resonances, settings, and recurring themes and images. As the poet himself said, "The characters in my poetry are found throughout my books; the principal themes intertwine, lianas connect the books, one to another….An evolution, yes, but concentric, starting from one central core."[viii] For the chronologically curious, we have appended a list of the texts in this volume in their order of publication (pp 146–147).

Our selections begin and end with rain. In the opening tale, "Noah's Ark," the watery wrath of God is in the detail. The Cosmic is personal: first felt by a diligent schoolgirl whose blotter has suddenly become so saturated that she cannot blot her homework. Inconsolable, she dissolves—literally—in tears. And so the Flood announces itself, with a combination of whimsy and bleakness that characterizes Supervielle's work. He sets "Noah's Ark" against the dark and sometimes brutal background of our mortality, and yet the story remains luminous with joy and jokes. The lion doesn't merely lie down with the lamb; he crushes his nose against the Ark's deck to block out her "exquisite scent" (under other circumstances, the smell of lunch). We readers can afford to laugh, in the midst of mayhem: the page floats us to safety.

From a series of water texts this collection moves on to dry land, leaving rivers and oceans behind for the pampas, then sailing into the spaciousness of biblical legend—and of the poet's own apartment in Paris, "so high up in space / Your wagons too, pulled by Percherons, one behind the other, / Their nostrils in eternity…" ("47 Boulevard Lannes").

The book's last text is "Raindrop," spoken like so many other of Supervielle's poems by God, but a God whose sense of helplessness matches our own. Elsewhere, he has promised us a gift: "I give you death because of its great compassion / And the infinity of all it contains" ("God Talks to Man"). But as we've suggested above, in Supervielle's universe this is a promise on which God isn't able to deliver fully; often, even when they want to, the dead don't "die completely" ("Unknown Girl of the Seine," "Child of the High Seas"). And here is the Creator, in "Raindrop," trying once again to do something he can't: to distinguish amidst all the water in the sea one drop of rain that just fell, "gleaming the length of its plummet." As created by Supervielle—his Catholic faith attenuated, though its myths remain with him to be rewritten—God can no more identify one raindrop than he can prevent human suffering. And he suffers just as we do from his failure, and asks our compassion:

> Pity your God, unable to make you happy,
> Little fragments of myself, O flickering sparks,
> I can offer you only a brazier where you can find fire again.
>
> ("God's Sorrow")

He cannot, as it turns out, "cure [us] of the flesh so inept at bearing pain" ("God Talks to Man").

Perhaps, however, in the brazier of language, fleetingly, the poet can.

—NANCY KLINE

---

i   Raymond, 328.

ii   Étiemble, 108.

iii   Supervielle, *Boire à la source [Drinking from the Source]*, in Étiemble, 158-9.

iv   Arland, 9.

v   See Hiddleston for an extended discussion of the equivalence between the pampas and the ocean, 30 ff.

vi   See "Perseus and Andromeda," trans. Patricia Terry and Nancy Kline, in *Essential Laforgue*.

vii   Étiemble, 34.

viii   Supervielle, cited in Étiemble, 41.

LIST OF WORKS CONSULTED:

Arland, Marcel. Préface, *Gravitations*. Jules Supervielle. Gallimard, 1966.

Caws, Mary Ann, ed. *The Yale Anthology of Twentieth-Century French Poetry*. Yale, 2004.

Étiemble, René. *Supervielle*. Gallimard, 1960.

Greene, Tatiana W. *Jules Supervielle*. Genève: Droz / Paris: Minard, 1958.

Hiddleston, James A. *L'Univers de Jules Supervielle*. Corti, 1965.

Orr, John, ed. Introduction, *Contes et poèmes*. Jules Supervielle. Edinburgh, 1950.

Raymond, Marcel. *De Baudelaire au Surréalisme*. Corti, 1966.

Terry, Patricia. *Essential Poems & Prose of Jules Laforgue*. Black Widow Press, 2010.

Vivier, Robert. *Lire Supervielle*. Corti, 1971.

SELECTED PROSE AND POETRY
OF JULES SUPERVIELLE

SELECTED PROSE AND POETRY

NOAH'S ARK

When she tried to blot her school exercises, a little girl from before the flood found her blotter wet through and through. This piece of paper dripped with water, even though its nature was to be perpetually thirsty! The child said to herself (she was by far the brightest pupil in her class) that perhaps the blotter was suffering from some marvelous disease. Because she was too poor to buy another, she put the pink sheet out to dry in the sun; but the blotter couldn't manage to rid itself of its distressing humidity. And meanwhile here's the ink on all her schoolwork also refusing to dry!

So, ashamed at being the object of a miracle that appeared to be meaningless, the child presented herself with a heavy heart before her schoolmistress's desk, holding the blotter in one hand and her notebook in the other, opened wide to the disobedient page. She couldn't have made herself clearer. And the mistress was obliged to watch her inconsolable student disappear before her very eyes, her whole being dissolved in tears.

Other misfortunes saddened the little town of Judea and its environs. Man's fire, which until now had been water's lustiest enemy, visibly began to fail. Stripped of its point and its passion, it did not dry out what came near it. People began to die here and there because they had water on the brain or in the belly. The tiniest blister on one finger signified a terminal inundation of the human body by noxious waters that little by little took the place of blood.

The same kind of aquatic delirium rapidly overtook the vegetable kingdom. Grass, leaves, branches and trunks oozed several times their weight in water in the course of a day. Everything did, even the grains of sand in the desert. There was no longer any relationship between the container and the contained, so huge was the wrath of God.

The town notables, whom no one could stop from sweating, finally wondered if this series of phenomena were not related to the flood so long predicted. But popular wisdom never tired of repeating: "As long as it doesn't rain, there's hope." At last, a raindrop landed on the mayor's head, bald by dint of scrutinizing the sky, and people had to understand that this was the end of everything. Not that it rained very hard that day, but in several places the rain had such soaking power that a few drops were enough to drown a peasant, his cart and his horse.

Noah hadn't waited for the flood to build his ark; he set it up with so much care and cunning that the rain avoided its vicinity, as though there were absolutely nothing to be done against it, no point in even trying.

The beasts chosen to be represented in Noah's vessel arrived two by two, sometimes from very far away. And these couples, happy to have escaped the great drenching, said to each other as they mounted the Ark: "And now, long live the Unknown!"

It smelled pretty intensely up there of wet fur; they were jammed onto the deck, and they vied for who could compress himself the most. You wondered by what miracle the elephant managed to fit into the corner where ordinarily there would scarcely have been room for a Newfoundland dog. And no matter where you turned, you witnessed edifying spectacles: a crocodile rocking in its affectionate jaws the head of a piglet sound asleep; tawny pelt and white wool negligently mingling like old childhood friends with nothing left to say to each other, who nonetheless delight in their proximity. And if the lion happened to lick the lamb, no one attributed it to *before-dinner* intentions. As for the lamb, unable to do any better, he held a little tuft of grass in his mouth which he treated with all kinds of consideration. Although the joy of animals is usually quite opaque, due to all the fur, feathers, and scales that usually encase it, all these beasts, completely at their ease, were radiant from head to tail.

On the wharf, many of those left behind tried to move Noah to pity. "Let us come aboard! We swear not to take up space." To which Noah responded: "What if the ark sank?!" "It won't sink! Cross our hearts!" cried thousands of the condemned. "Be well!" was Noah's reply.

Certain people went at it more subtly, in their attempt to get on board. As witness a family of acrobats in pink tights, faded by the bad weather. Known throughout the region—but what becomes of celebrity in flooded lands!—now they were counting on nothing more than their acts of daring to touch the hearts of those more fortunate in this world, those about to sail off in the Ark. Before the wondrously diverse heads of the passengers along the ship's railing, the acrobats built and dismantled, only to build again, a human pyramid crowned by a girl, three years of age, already as skillful as her grandfather who served as the foundation of the entire edifice.

And there occurred—at the command "Upsadaisy," "Look lively," or "Take it slow"—back-breaking leaps, incredible but perfect somersaults.

And what to say of the wet handkerchief they threw each other, with which they pretended to wipe their streaming but capable hands.

And always on the lips of these athletes of all sizes, a smile of perfect courtesy, never obsequious, strictly professional.

"Let them up! Let them up! They'll entertain us during the trip," the passengers cried. "Look at the little girl, how adorable she is!" Noah felt even the beams of his Ark, chosen for their inflexibility, begin to soften with dangerous pity beneath his feet, but on board there was only space enough for regret and its uncontrollable weight. Then, his heart in tears but his eyes dry, he gave the order to cast off, abandoning the tireless members of this very muscular family, which momentum caused to continue leaping up over each other. Water from the heavens wasn't slow to do them favors: at least it erased them at one fell swoop from the list of the living. But for a long time all those who leaned over the ship's rail believed they saw them perform their feats again and again at the bottom of the water.

Since certain animals were not to be represented in the Ark, Noah hadn't hesitated to give them the wrong hour of departure. The gangway had already risen when a megatherium presented itself:

"If your name is Noah, you don't forget anyone!" he cried, conscious of his enormous strength.

"It's not a question of forgetting," said the father of the Ark, sorrowfully. "Your destiny is to be antediluvian. Well, the deluge has begun: who would dare argue to the contrary?"

"That *I* am not represented among the animals in the Ark—*me*, the biggest of them all! It's scandalous. Because of you, Noah, one day it won't even be known that I lived!"

"Cheer up, my great big friend, they'll know you by your vertebrae."

The Ark was pulling away ever faster, its doors closed, the megatherium dashing in pursuit, and, even more than its massive clumsiness, its rage sent it rapidly to the bottom of the waters.

Then a group of antediluvians joined forces to batter Noah's vessel, which they tried in vain to capsize. They asked the whale to join them, but being orthodox and certain of surviving, she quickly swam off with her calves, instructing them, "Don't turn around, those are anarchists."

There still remained a great many living creatures who were strong swimmers, and they surrounded the seafaring Ark with their cries. In the brotherhood of those condemned to die, you saw greenish animals and humans jumbled up together, islets scarcely afloat, in the grip of swirling eddies. A woman in her sixties was swimming—for the first time in her life—not far from a ten-pointed stag; three Jews screamed on a passing hippopotamus. Boats capsized without apparent cause: it was the flood taking hold of them from underneath, with its huge rainwater hand, and emptying them in the twinkling of an eye.

And a hummingbird sobbed:

> *I am a bird of the islands*
> *Swallowed up by the sea.*
> *Ah! what's to become of me!*

"Make way, make way. I'm the father of twelve children," announced a man on a raft who still believed in justice.

"Look, you have to be reasonable," cried Noah, leaning over the railing.

"Reasonable! What does that mean?" more than a thousand voices answered.

But as there was no response, the floating animals clamored for the lion, up on the balcony. His head appeared over the railing.

"Speak up, give us reasons," they shouted at him from every direction. "Why you and not us?"

The king of all the animals, whether they were drowning or not, said sadly but firmly: "What must be must be."

"Must be *what?* Come tell that to us in the water, if you have a grain of courage."

"Aren't I worth more than the snake who's on board?" said a dove, whose rage made her resemble a tiger in the prime of life.

"What must be must be," the lion repeated, ashamed to have no other argument.

At last the very poverty of this dialectic discouraged the questioners. It was fate. Nothing for it but to consent to drink the gloomy water that cruelly offered its services everywhere.

For a long time the sea continued to be infested with supplicants and Noah blushed to think he wouldn't be able to get to sleep until not a single thing remained alive around the Ark.

The last of the survivors was undoubtedly the swimmer, gigantic from head to toe, who overtook the Ark in the middle of the sea. Noah was about to stop his ears, when the man cried: "Don't worry about me, I'll make it! You know, I could stay for weeks in the water. I've always been a success before, and a little bit of rain isn't going to persuade me that I wasn't born under a lucky star. Always cheerful too, you know. Ah, I pity you being stuck in your cage. I'm telling you: Long Live Freedom!" And he kicked expansively in the water to show he wasn't lacking for room.

"After all," they began to murmur on the Ark, "why shouldn't he survive? He's certainly earned it. No one in Noah's family can compare with his physical and intellectual resources. Shem can't even swim, and as for Japheth, the only thing that interests him on board is arranging the animals by size, all up and down the deck, which needlessly irritates everybody, or just about."

The next day Noah was not too surprised to find the man following his ship. Not knowing what to do with this inveterate swimmer, he sometimes threw him a piece of meat surreptitiously, in the middle of the night. All the animals did more or less the same, to such a degree that the man was gaining weight in the tepid water.

And who would have taken it on himself to abandon this solitary figure in the middle of the deep? Even the cruelest God would have retreated before such confidence in the life that He had given him.

An enormous shark who obviously belonged to the silent flood police approached the swimmer and rolled over to examine him with the eyes on the underside of his head. Then moved away without a reproach, but signalled to an angel, who tapped the swimmer's head lightly with her wand. Beneath her touch, the man split into two equal and painless halves, which became a couple of porpoises. Such was the origin of these fish, who are always in a good mood and, unreconciled to living entirely at sea, pop up from time to time to see what's happening in the world of ships and men.

As the land masses disappeared one by one beneath water from the heavens, Noah scanned the horizon so that he might head toward what sailors usually avoid: mountains. But the rain did its work so fast that the Flood always beat him to the summit.

The Ark, at any rate, progressed like a well-cleaned and caulked vessel: all those who had been hanging on to her had long since let go. Nothing more floated around the ship than a faceless anguish, and on board they talked about how fortunate fish were…

Just a few hours after departure, Noah saw a monkey scratch himself and understood that there were stowaways in the Ark.

"Creatures, no matter how small," said he, "must travel separately. I don't want any parasites aboard, got that?"

"Not even two miserable little fleas?" asked a dog. "We are as one."

Noah made the animals on the Ark step into a walk-in cupboard. There, anything extra threw off a bright light and died instantly and hygienically.

During the first hours of the crossing, all eyes were on the short-lived insects—with somewhat perverse curiosity, it must be admitted. They were expected to expire in front of everybody. But the next day all were obliged to congratulate them: they were still alive.

Noah explained this miracle from the bridge: the Ark was so cleverly constructed that it conferred health on all those to be found there.

"Nothing to be so proud of!" muttered his wife, in an aside. "You could have made it bigger, your Ark! Every time you want to turn around on deck, you have to ask permission from twenty different animals!"

Nonetheless each felt so good about himself that he had to put it to the test. Japheth hopped all day long on one foot without feeling the least bit tired and advised everyone, even the quadrupeds, to imitate him. As for Noah's daughters, they pinched themselves black and blue without so much as a twinge of pain.

Having nothing to do on board, the animals thought only about eating. A strange nervous hunger agitated all of them, each judging that his ration was altogether insufficient. And it must be recognized that Noah, fearing there would be no room, had skimped.

First and foremost among the malcontents came the omnivores. They claimed, by right, a taste of everything that could be eaten. And how could Noah have remembered everything, even if only a taste were required? This was a metaphysical problem, not an alimentary one.

So much famished proximity on deck! Would it not all end with the most horrible of bloodbaths, a cubbyhole massacre? The great beasts began to consider the others with a less than frank gaze. Their misty tenderness signified not so much love as horrible preferences for such and such a part of one's fellow creature: haunch, fillet or loin with kidneys.

Already the lion lay with his nose crushed against the deck so as not to smell the exquisite scent of his neighbor, uncooked lamb. Already a Saint Bernard, known for his great purity from frequenting the snows, was asking for a muzzle, which a passing angel instantly attached in front of everybody, to set an example. But the wolf thought these scenes ridiculous.

"Hunger," he said, "is only satisfied with meat, preferably alive!"

"Come, come, no need for it to be alive," said the lion, whose noble sentiments were still of this world.

"Hunger is hunger," replied the wolf. "It causes revolutions."

"There's an excellent way to forget your hunger," said the camel, who rarely ate. "Chew on a little piece of wood."

"What leads to first-rate results," added the snake, "is to focus your thinking energetically on the smell of vomit."

"Well, I'd eat vomit!" said the wolf. "That's how bad it's gotten. Meanwhile, everybody watch your skin!"

The lion, who had no difficulty in assembling everyone, took the floor: "My friends, let us choose examples from among ourselves and remain calm. What does the lizard do in battle? He gives up his tail to conserve the better part of his strength. A great lesson! Are there not many among us whose bodies offer parts condemned in advance because they aren't really vital? Why has the squirrel got a tail almost as big as himself, which follows him around like a reproach? What does the sow do with so many teats? Is she certain she couldn't spare half of them?"

"She is perfectly certain," says the sow from her spot.

"Let her look to her conscience!"

"Her conscience is perfectly at peace."

"We'll see about that," says the lion, altogether unruffled.

And everyone thought to himself: "Well, *I* have absolutely nothing to spare. I'm very fond of everything about me."

"On certain of our beloved brethren," the lion continued, "we would also find one or two pounds of meat that are not indispensable to them."

"And you, how come you've got such a big head?" blurted out an enormous bear who had kept silent until then.

"It's crucial that I have enough room to think of each of you," answered the lion. "But to show you my spirit of sacrifice, I am placing at your disposition—all of you, big and small, starting with the smallest—my royal mane."

A great burst of laughter, and the lion crestfallen: "You hurt me deeply," he said, scarcely holding back the tears that came to him, who knew how? from his neighbor the crocodile.

But his speech was interrupted by the cheers that greeted angels bearing baskets of supplies. Yes, everything would have been for the best, were it not for the never-ending rain. Not a dry second, 24/7. This, because Earth and its men had caused Heaven such enormous suffering! And how could Noah, with his skinny crew, console the whole celestial vault?

Sometimes the shadows lightened a little and you thought the sky was going to grow more peaceful. But its tears picked up again, harder than ever, without the least thought for the consequences.

One day, at last, it seemed the firmament was making a desperate attempt to smile through its tears. A certain light, gray at first, grew sharper—and suddenly all the colors of beautiful weather clustered there: the Rainbow!

But this represented no advance; the waters went on rising as if they proposed to reach the sky and give it a taste of its own medicine.

And Noah, a good captain, worried to see the shrinking space between him and the universal ceiling.

Each creature in the Ark was thinking: *Something must be done! Something must absolutely be done! But what?*

"Trust me!" bellowed Noah from the bridge.

But his heart was in his boots and to show the good Lord the depth of his anguish he secretly sent Him the blackest thing he had on board: a crow.

The bird left, never to return.

"What a dumb idea, anyway, sending a crow! The battle was already lost," said Noah's wife, who'd seen him release the bird.

And both of them at the same time reached their hands out toward a dove whose whiteness and trust in the future were so great they must have come down through the centuries to us.

Noah seized the bird and murmured in her ear: "Earth! Earth! Earth!" in the hope of making her a carrier pigeon.

The dove soared straight ahead of her and didn't return until the next day, to land on the captain's broad shoulders. We know that she was holding an olive branch in her beak.

The waters had begun to sink and Noah directed his ship toward the rainbow, hoping against hope that something like earth would finally emerge.

One day at last, at dawn, the rainbow haloed Mount Ararat. And as they neared, they saw a kind of gaiety on all the mountain's face, which in ordinary times was untamed and repellent. With its rocky raucous voice it cried out to the animals on the Ark:

"This way, look at me, I am a mountain of good will! And you, the animals, what have you been doing all this time? We thought we'd be obliged to do without animals. We were already picturing furry four-legged trees."

When the Ark had docked, Noah made his passengers advance, two by two, down the gangway, starting with the most fragile. But having reached the middle of the plank from which they must soar to Earth, two mayflies stopped, immobilized.

"Let's go, fly off!" their captain shouted at them. "Don't you see we've arrived? Who stuck me with such oafish insects!"

But they remained absolutely immobile. And already the father of the Ark was brandishing his hat, and everyone understood that he was mortal again.

"Bring on the reserve mayflies!" said Noah, in the tearless voice of authority.

Still stunned by the smell of Earth, which went to their heads like new wine, the insects hesitated for an instant, then all at once sprang forward and landed safely on Mount Ararat, to the cheering of the crowd.

"Come, come, quiet please!" cried Noah. "We're not at the theatre…. Quick, send the next ones down. We don't have a minute to lose."

NK

GENÈSE

Encore ruisselant du jour qu'il venait de créer,
Comme celui qui est pour la première fois éclairé par une lumière
    extérieure à lui,
Dieu parcourait le monde de son pas de commandement,
Suivi à distance respectueuse par un soleil luisant de gratitude.
Et le soleil considérait les mains qui l'avaient sorti de l'ombre,
Il les trouvait à son goût.
Et la joie des choses créées sonnait si juste
Qu'on eût dit que chacun venait d'inventer ses propres couleurs
Et l'herbe était verte et le ciel bleu, les nuages blancs et obscurs,
L'arc-en-ciel luisait de toutes les couleurs à la fois!
Et chacun à travers les âges devait garder sa robe neuve du premier jour,
Et malgré sa taille humaine
Dieu pouvait se pencher sans effort sur les monts immenses et les vallées,
Il était toujours à l'échelle.
Le grand et le petit, le long et le large disparaissaient rapidement dans son
    harmonie;
Et le soleil se coucha pour la première fois,
Afin de laisser la place à une nuit chaleureuse, suante de signes et de
    prodiges,
Et qui sursautait dans ses ténèbres et dans ses profondeurs, encore de nos
    jours en gestation.
Dieu avait fait une nuit si vivante d'étoiles qu'il en marchait un peu
    voûté, mais fièrement,
Et tout ce qu'il n'avait pu créer de ses mains, il le façonnait de sa pensée
    qui restait créatrice à des distances infinies;
Et sa pensée fourbue d'avoir tant procréé au loin
Rentrait parfois au bercail.
Et Dieu songea tout d'un coup: Et ma mer qui est vide!
Alors il se cacha la tête dans l'eau salée et toute la mer aussitôt en devint
    poissonneuse,
Et les marsouins firent des bonds à la surface,
La baleine lança son jet d'eau,

GENESIS

Still shimmering with the day he had just created,
Illuminated for the first time by light from outside himself,
God traveled the world with his commanding stride,
Followed at a respectful distance by the sun shining with gratitude.
And the sun considered the hands which had drawn it out of the
    shadows,
And found them pleasing.
The joy of the newly created things was so perfect
Each one seemed to have just invented its own colors
And the grass was green and the sky blue, the clouds white or dark,
The rainbow gleamed with all its colors at once!
And each of them, forever, was to be dressed as on the first day
And in spite of his human dimensions
God could effortlessly lean down over the immensity of the mountains
    and the valleys,
His size was always right.
The large and the small, the long and the wide were quickly absorbed in
    his harmony.
And the sun set for the first time
In order to leave room for a warm night oozing with portents and
    marvels,
Leaping within its shadows and in its depths still today giving birth.
God had made a night so alive with stars that he walked with his back
    bent slightly but proudly
And everything he couldn't create with his hands he formed in his
    mind, creative over infinite distances
And his thought exhausted from having created so much so far away
Sometimes returned to the fold.
And God suddenly thought, "But my seas are empty!"
And he hid his face in the salt water and the whole sea was suddenly full
    of fish
And dolphins were bounding over the surface,
And the whale hurled its stream of water upward

Car la joie était pour chacun un secret mal gardé!

L'air essayait les oiseaux et les oiseaux, l'air,

Ils comprirent sur-le-champ qu'ils étaient faits l'un pour l'autre.

Et le cheval et le taureau entraient également dans l'air,

Et la girafe et le rhinocéros et les agneaux de trois jours ne cessaient de le fréquenter,

Car l'air était à tout le monde sans qu'on eût besoin de se le partager.

Et pour avoir quelqu'un à qui parler de ce qu'il avait façonné, Dieu fit l'homme.

Et les visages neufs des enfants étaient des réponses,

Et ceux usés des hommes et des femmes en étaient d'autres,

Et les roses avec leurs pétales très silencieux étaient des réponses à des questions que nous ignorons encore,

Et les arbres chevelus et les monts chauves et glâcés,

Et l'herbe!

Les questions ont disparu et les réponses sont restées aussi fraîches et catégoriques qu'au premier jour.

Et la face du lion avec sa barbe circulaire était aussi une réponse,

Et c'est maintenant un hiéroglyphe dont nous ne parvenons pas à faire le tour et qu'il nous faut déchiffrer avec soin.

Et la haute stature de la girafe aussi bien que le tremblement du tremble ou les glands du chêne et les écureuils!

Et Dieu se révéla toute de suite comme un grand peintre de paysages aux perspectives sans fin et qui ne voulaient rien savoir d'un cadre,

Un peintre de portraits en pied autour desquels on pouvait tourner, et si ressemblants

Qu'ils en étaient doués de la parole et des larmes.

Océan Atlantique, 8-13 juillet 46

Not one of them could keep the secret of its joy!
The air tried out birds and birds the air,
At once they understood they were made for each other
And the horse and the bull also entered the air
And the giraffe and the rhinoceros and the three-day old lamb took part
in it too
For the air belonged to everyone, no need to divide it up.
And in order to have someone to talk with about what he had made,
God created human beings
And the new faces of the children were answers
And the tired faces of men and women were others
And the roses with their very quiet petals were answers to questions we
haven't thought of yet
And the leafy trees and the bald and frozen mountains
And the grass!
The questions have disappeared and the answers have remained as fresh
and uncompromising as on the first day.
And the lion's face with its circular beard was also a response
And now it's a hieroglyphic we never get to the end of and have to
interpret with care,
And the height of the giraffe and the trembling of the aspen or acorns
from the oak trees and the squirrels!
And God revealed himself right away as a great painter of landscapes
whose spaces are boundless and not at all interested in frames,
A painter of full-length portraits you could walk around, and so realistic
They could speak and shed tears.

Atlantic Ocean, July 8–13, 1946

PT & KM

I always assumed you stayed on the bottom of the river, but I'm floating up. So thought the nineteen-year-old drowned girl, confusedly, quite out of her depth.

It was just beyond the Alexandre Bridge that she had a terrible fright: the cruel agents of the River Police knocked her on the shoulder with their boathooks, trying unsuccessfully to catch hold of her dress.

Happily, night was falling and they gave up.

Imagine being fished back! she thought. *Having to lie exposed in front of those people on a slab in some morgue, unable to make the slightest movement to defend yourself or back away, unable even to lift your little finger. Feeling yourself dead, as they stroke your leg. And not one woman, not one woman to dry you off, then bathe and dress you one last time.*

She had now finally wended her way out of Paris and was spooling along between banks embellished with trees and pastures, trying to catch herself by day in some bend in the river, so that she might travel at night when the moon and stars came one by one to rub themselves against the scales of fishes.

If only I could reach the sea, I who no longer fear the highest wave.

She traveled without knowing that a tremulous smile shone on her face, so much more resistant than the smile of a living woman, always at the mercy of no matter what.

To reach the sea: these words now kept her company in the river.

Eyelids closed, feet together, arms moving as the water wished, annoyed at how one of her stockings was bunching right below the knee, her throat still trying to draw strength from life's domain, she advanced, a floating minor news item, knowing no other pace than that of France's ancient river, which always took the same meanderings as it proceeded blindly to-ward the sea.

Passing through a town (*Am I in Mantes, am I in Rouën?*) she was caught for a few instants in an eddy that wedged her against the arch of a bridge, and a tugboat had to chug close by her, stirring up the water, to get her underway again.

I'll never ever reach the sea, she thought, deep in the heart of her third night underwater.

"But that's exactly where you are," said a man close up beside her, who she could just make out was very tall, and naked. He attached a lead weight to her ankle.

Then he took her hand with such authority, so persuasively that she might not have resisted even if she had not been a small dead girl.

Let's rely on him. I who can no longer do anything for myself.

And the young girl's body was bathed in deeper and deeper water.

When they had reached the sands that wait beneath the sea, several phosphorescent creatures came toward them, but the man, who was the "Great Watery One," dispersed them with a gesture.

"Trust us," he said to the girl. "The mistake, you see, is to try to keep on breathing. Don't be scared to feel a heart inside you that hardly beats anymore, and then only by mistake. And don't press your lips together like that, as if you were afraid to swallow ocean water. For you, it is now what fresh water once was. You have nothing more to fear, you understand, nothing more to fear. Do you feel your strength returning?"

"Ah, I'm going to faint!"

"Not on your life. To speed up the process of adjustment, pour some of the fine sand at your feet from one hand to the other. No point in rushing. Like that, yes. You'll get your balance back right away."

She recovered full consciousness. But suddenly she grew terribly afraid again. How was it that she understood this sailor of the abyss without his pronouncing a single word in all this water? Her fear, however, was short-lived: she realized that the man expressed himself just with his body's phosphorescence. Even her own bare and weightless arms gave off responses in the form of tiny lights like fireflies. And the Streaming Creatures around them made themselves understood in precisely the same way.

"And now may I know where you come from?" asked The Great Watery One, keeping his profile to her, as was the custom among the Streaming Creatures whenever a man addressed a young girl.

"I no longer know anything about myself, not even my name."

"Well, you'll be the Unknown Girl of the Seine, that's all. Believe me, we are scarcely more knowledgeable about ourselves. Just know that this is a large colony of Streaming Creatures and that you won't be unhappy here."

She was blinking rapidly, as people do when bothered by too bright a light, and the Great Watery One waved away all but one of the torch fish.

Indeed, these creatures shone everywhere around them, lighting up the depths, immobile.

People of all ages were approaching now, out of curiosity. They were naked.

"Do you have any requests?" asked the Great Watery One.

"I'd like to keep my dress on."

"You will, young lady. It's that simple."

And in the eyes, in the slow and courteous gestures of the inhabitants of the depths, you could see a genuine desire to be of service to the new-comer.

The lead weight attached to her leg bothered her. She planned to rid herself of it, or at the very least to untie the knot, the minute she was out of sight. The Great Watery One understood her intentions.

"Above all, don't touch that. Please. You would lose consciousness and float to the surface—if, somehow, you managed to clear the great shark barrier."

The young girl resigned herself and, imitating those around her, started waving away algae and fish. There were many extremely curious little fish who hovered like flies or mosquitos around her face and body, some-times even touching her.

One or two (rarely three) fat domestic fish or guard fish devoted them-selves to every Streaming Creature and helped them out in little ways, as for example holding various objects in their mouths or scrubbing your back of the marine grasses that got stuck there. They came rushing over at the slightest gesture, or even before. At times their obsequiousness was irritating. But all the same, you saw a round simplistic admiration in their eyes that was a pleasure. And never did they eat the other little fishes in service like themselves.

Why did I throw myself in the water? wondered the newcomer. *I don't even know if I was a grown woman or a girl up there. The only thing in my head is algae and shellfish. And I have a great desire to say it's all very <u>sad</u>, although I'm really no longer sure what that word means.*

Seeing her so upset, another young girl came over who'd been ship-wrecked two years before, and who was called the Natural One:

"Staying down here in the depths," she said, "will really build your confidence—just you wait. But you have to give your flesh time to reshape itself, to get dense enough so that your body won't float back to the surface.

And won't constantly be wanting food and drink. Such childishness wears off fast. And I'll bet that soon real pearls will fall from your eyes, just when you least expect it. That will be the first sign that you're acclimating."

"What do people do here?" asked the Unknown Girl of the Seine, after a moment.

"A thousand things. We're never bored, I promise you. We visit the bottom of the sea to welcome isolated beings and bring them here, so as to build the strength of our colony. What a feeling when we find one who believes himself condemned eternally to solitude in our huge crystal prison! How he staggers and hangs on to underwater plants! How he conceals himself! He thinks he sees sharks everywhere. And then here comes a man like him, who takes him in his arms—as nurses do after a battle—to carry him toward regions where he will have nothing more to fear."

"And sinking ships? Do you often see them?"

"Only once. I saw thousands and thousands of things meant for the surface drifting to the bottom of the sea. Everything landing on top of us, tumbling around in the water: dishes, trunks, rigging, even baby carriages. We had to go help those who were trapped in their cabins—first of all, to remove their life belts. Streaming Creatures, ax in hand, worked energetically to free the shipwrecked. Then, hiding their axes, did their best to reassure them. We stored all the different provisions in warehouses underneath our territory, which is underneath the sea."

"But since no one needs anything—?"

"We pretend to, so the time will weigh less heavily."

A man came forward, leading a horse by its bridle. The resplendent beast approached obliquely, shining with a majesty, a courtesy, an acceptance of death that were so many marvels. And all the quicksilver bubbles rising around his body!

"We have very few horses," said the Natural One. "They are a great luxury here."

Near the Unknown Girl of the Seine the man halted the beast, which bore a sidesaddle. "From the Great Watery One," he said.

"Oh my! I hope he'll forgive me, but I just don't feel up to it yet."

And the beautiful rejected horse turned from her in all his elegance and splendor as if nothing in the world could change him or move him.

"The Great Watery One is in command here?" asked the Unknown Girl of the Seine, who felt sure he was.

"Yes, he's the strongest of us all and the one who knows the region best. And so solid that he can go up almost the whole way to the surface. Some fools even claim he is in contact with the sun, the stars and men. But there's nothing to that. And it's wonderful enough that he can rise to meet drowned wanderers. Yes, he's one of those beings completely unknown on earth who have achieved celebrity under the sea. You won't find a trace in history, as it's taught up there, of the French admiral Bernard de la Michelette, or his wife Pristine, or our Great Watery One, who drowned when he was a simple cabin boy at the age of twelve and was so much at home in the underwater world that he grew here to awe-inspiring proportions and became a giant among our fauna."

The Unknown Girl of the Seine never took off her dress, not even to sleep; it was the only thing she'd salvaged from her previous life. She made the most of the garment's folds and moisture, which lent her a miraculous elegance in the midst of so many women stripped of their clothes. And the men would very much have liked to know the curve of her breasts.

As a way of asking forgiveness for her dress, the young girl lived apart, with a modesty that was perhaps a little too conspicuous, and she spent her days gathering seashells for the children or the humble or the most badly maimed among the drowned. She was always the first to say hello and often apologized, even when there was no reason.

Each day the Great Watery One paid her a visit, and there they hovered, the two of them, shimmering in their phosphorescence like fragments of the Milky Way, stretched out chastely side by side.

"We can't be far from the coast," she said one day. "If only I could get back up the river to hear a few city sounds, even just the bell of a trolley that's running late, in the middle of the night."

"Poor child, your memory fails you: are you forgetting that you're dead and up there you would run the risk of being shut away in the most odious of prisons? The living don't like it when we roam, and they quickly punish us for our wanderings. Here you're free, sheltered."

"What about you? Don't you ever think of the things up there? They often come to me, one by one, in no particular order, which makes me very unhappy. Right now, I see an oak table, well-polished but all by itself. It vanishes and here's the eye of a rabbit. And now it's the print of an ox's hoof in the sand. All this seems to approach me on some kind of mission, yet announces nothing but its presence. And whenever things come to me

SELECTED PROSE AND POETRY

in pairs, they don't belong together. Here, I see a cherry steeped in lake water. And what am I to make of this seagull in a bed, this partridge perched on the glass chimney of a huge smoking lamp? I don't know anything more hopeless. These fragments of life, without life—is that what's meant by death?"

And she added, for her ears alone:

"And you yourself, so close to me here, in profile, like a warrior carved out of ice?"

One after another, mothers refused to let their daughters associate with the Unknown Girl of the Seine, because of the dress she wore day and night.

A shipwrecked woman whose reason had been shattered even after death and who could find no peace said:

"She's *alive*. I'm telling you that girl is alive. If she were like us, it wouldn't matter to her not to wear a dress. Such ornaments have nothing to do with the dead."

"Oh, keep quiet. You're out of your head," said the Natural One. "How can you claim she's alive, under the sea?"

"It's true you can't live under the sea," answered the madwoman, stricken, as though she were suddenly remembering a lesson learned very long ago.

But that didn't stop her from coming back soon afterwards to repeat:

"I'm here to tell you she's alive!"

"Would you leave us alone, you crackpot," the Natural One replied. "Really, people shouldn't be allowed to say such things!"

But even she who had been the Unknown Girl's best friend approached her one day with a face that seemed to say *I too hold this against you*.

"Why are you clinging to a dress, at the bottom of the sea?" said the Natural One.

"I feel as if it shelters me from all I don't yet understand."

Then a woman who had reproached her before cried:

"She's all too happy to call attention to herself that way. She's nothing but a little slut. And I assure you if I'd been a mother on earth and my daughter was with me now, I wouldn't hesitate to say to her: *Take off that dress, you hear me?!* And that goes for you too—take it off!" she said to the Unknown Girl, addressing her familiarly in order to humiliate her. (This was the worst of insults, at the bottom of the sea.) "Otherwise, watch out for these, Sweetheart!" she said, brandishing a pair of scissors, which she finally threw at the young girl's feet, enraged.

"Will you get lost!" said the Natural One, upset by so much spite.

Left alone, the Unknown Girl hid her pain as best she could, in the heavy and difficult water.

Isn't that what's called envy, she thought, *on earth?*

And seeing heavy pearls fall sadly from her eyes:

"Ah, no! Never!" she said. "I cannot, I do not want to get adjusted."

She escaped in the direction of deserted regions, just as fast as would permit the lead weight she was dragging with her leg.

You dreadful semblances of life, she thought, *leave me in peace. Just leave me be! What am I supposed to do with you, now that the rest is gone!*

When she had left all the torch fish far behind her and she found herself in deepest dark, she cut the steel cord that attached her to the bottom of the sea, using the black scissors she'd picked up before escaping.

At last to die completely, she thought, rising through the water.

In the oceanic night her phosphorescence grew intensely luminous, then went out forever. The smile of a wandering drowned girl curved on her lips again. And her favorite fishes didn't hesitate to go with her—I mean to die by suffocation—as she reached the shallow water.

NK

UN POÈTE

Je ne vais pas toujours seul au fond de moi-même
Et j'entraîne avec moi plus d'un être vivant.
Ceux qui seront entrés dans mes froides cavernes
Sont-ils sûrs d'en sortir même pour un moment?
J'entasse dans ma nuit, comme un vaisseau qui sombre,
Pêle-mêle, les passagers et les marins,
Et j'éteins la lumière aux yeux, dans les cabines,
Je me fais des amis des grandes profondeurs.

A POET

I don't always go alone to the bottom of my self,
Quite often living captives keep me company.
Those who have stepped inside my cold caverns,
Are they sure that they can ever leave again?
Like a sinking ship I pile up in my night
Pell-mell all the passengers and sailors,
Then I extinguish all the cabin lights;
The great depths will come to be my friends.

PT & KM

POINTE DE FLAMME

Tout le long de sa vie
Il avait aimé à lire
Avec une bougie
Et souvent il passait
La main dessus la flamme
Pour se persuader
Qu'il vivait,
Qu'il vivait.

Depuis le jour de sa mort
Il tient à côté de lui
Une bougie allumée
Mais garde les mains cachées.

FLAME TIP

All during his life
He had preferred to read
By candlelight
And often he would place
His hand over the flame
In order to be sure
He was alive,
Alive.

Since the day of his death
He keeps near him
A lighted candle
But his hands are hidden.

PT & KM

DIEU PARLE À L'HOMME

Quand je dis "mes bras" ne va pas croire
Que ce sont des bras comme les tiens,
Quand je dis "mes yeux" comprends que rien
Ni autour de toi, ni la mémoire
Ne t'en révèle un seul regard.
Je me sers des mots qui sont à toi.

    Si tu ne me saisis pas bien
    Restons taciturnes ensemble.
    Que mon secret touche le tien,
    Que ton silence me ressemble.

★

Moi qui suis l'univers et ne peux en jouir
Puisque tout est en moi dans sa masse importune,
Je te ferai présent des choses une à une
Puisqu'il te suffira de voir pour les cueillir.
Ainsi garderas-tu même ce qui m'échappe,
Ce qui ne m'est plus rien tu pourras le tenir
Et suivre vivement d'un regard qui rattrape
L'hirondelle en son vol ou retrant à son nid.

★

Je te donne la mort avec une espérance
Ne me demande pas de te la définir,
Je te donne la mort avec la différence
Entre un passé chétif et mieux que l'avenir,
Je te donne la mort pour sa grande clémence
Et tout son contenu qui ne peut pas finir.
Bientôt, petit, bientôt, tu seras un mort libre

GOD TALKS TO MAN

When I say "my arms" don't imagine
Arms like your own,
When I say "my eyes" understand that nothing
Either close to you or in your memory
Will reveal even a single one of my glances.
The words I am using are yours.

If you don't grasp what I say
Let us both remain quiet,
May my secret touch yours,
Your silence be like me.

★

I can take no delight in the universe — it is myself;
I bear the weight of everything that exists,
From which I'll select for you, one by one, gifts
Which you can receive just by opening your eyes.
You will keep even what escapes me —
Nothing to me now — it will be yours,
Your sight will be keen enough to arrest
The swallow's flight or the return to her nest.

★

I give you death with a hope —
Don't ask me to define it,
I give you death with the difference
Between a meager past and the imperfect future,
I give you death because of its great compassion
And the infinity of all it contains.
Soon, my little one, soon you'll be dead and free,

Tu te reconnaîtras entier et fibre à fibre
Sans le secours des yeux qui pouvaient bien périr,
Bientôt tu parcourras les plus grandes distances
Dans l'immobilité du corps et le silence,
Laisse-moi faire et je promets de te guérir
De la chair malhabile à porter la souffrance.

You will know yourself as a whole and in detail
Without the help of the eyes you won't retain,
Soon you will travel the vast reaches of space
In silence and immobility,
Trust me and I promise to cure you
Of the flesh so inept at bearing pain.

PT & KM

How had this floating street been formed? What sailors, helped by what architects, constructed it, in the middle of the Atlantic, on the surface of the sea, above a chasm six thousand meters deep? This long street with its red brick houses, faded to a silvery French gray, these roofs of slate, of tile, these humble unchanging shops? And this intricate openwork steeple? This fenced-in plot of ocean water, clearly meant to be a garden, enclosed by walls bristling with broken glass, over which there jumped, from time to time, a fish?

How did it remain upright, not even bobbing in the waves?

And this twelve-year-old child, so alone, who walked along the liquid street in clogs, as surefooted as if she were walking on dry land? How had this come to pass…?

We will explain things gradually, as we see and understand them. And what must remain inexplicable, in spite of us, will.

When a ship approached, before it even appeared on the horizon, the child fell into a deep sleep and the village disappeared beneath the waves. And this is the reason that no sailor, not even through his telescope, had ever noticed it, nor suspected its existence.

The child thought herself the only little girl in the world. Did she even know she was a little girl?

She wasn't remarkably pretty, because of the spaces between her teeth and her slightly upturned nose, but her skin was very white and sweetly speckled, I mean freckled. And her little person, dominated by modest but very luminous gray eyes, struck you to the bottom of your soul with a sense of wonder arising from the depths of time.

In the street, the only street in this little town, the child sometimes looked to right and left, as if she were expecting someone to wave or nod or offer some sign of friendship. Simply an impression she gave, unknowingly, since nothing and no one could ever come to this lost village, always poised and ready to disappear.

What did she live on? Fish? We don't think so. She found food, even meat every two or three days, in the kitchen cupboard and the pantry. There were also potatoes for her, some other vegetables, eggs from time to time.

Provisions appeared spontaneously in the cupboards. And when the child took some jam out of a jar, it remained no less full, as if things had once been this way and must remain so eternally.

In the morning half a loaf of fresh bread, wrapped in paper, awaited the child on the marble bakery counter, behind which she'd never seen anyone, not even a hand, a finger, pushing the bread toward her.

Up early, she raised the metal louvers on the shops (here you read Café & Bar; there, Blacksmith, Modern Bakery, Haberdashery), unhooked the shutters on all the houses, fastened them carefully against the sea wind and, depending on the weather, left the windows open or closed. In several kitchens she lit a fire so that smoke rose above three or four rooftops.

One hour before sunset, she matter-of-factly started closing shutters. And she lowered the corrugated iron louvers.

The child accomplished these tasks motivated by some instinct, some day-to-day inspiration that caused her to take care of everything. In the right season, she aired a rug at the window or left laundry out to dry, as though it were necessary that the village seem, as convincingly as possible, inhabited.

And all year long, she had to take care of the flag outside city hall, so exposed to the elements.

At night, she lit candles or sewed by lamplight. There was also electricity in several houses in the village, and the child switched it on and off with artless grace.

Once, she knotted black crepe on the knocker of a front door. She liked the way that looked.

And it remained there for two days, after which she took it down.

Another time, there she was in the street, beating the drum, the village drum, as though to announce some piece of news. And she had a violent urge to shout something that would be heard from one end of the sea to the other, but her throat closed and she could make no sound. She tried so hard that her face and neck went almost black, like the drowned. Then she had to put the drum away in its habitual place, in the lefthand corner at the back of the big room in the city hall.

The child climbed up the steeple on a spiral staircase, its steps worn away by thousands of never-seen feet. The steeple, which the child thought must be five hundred steps high (it was ninety-two), showed as much sky as it could between its yellow bricks. And you had to coddle the clock, with its weights, by cranking it up, so it would truly ring the hours, day and night.

The crypt, the altars, the stone saints giving tacit orders, all the scarcely whispering chairs, neatly lined up and awaiting beings from all the ages, the altars whose gold had aged and would gladly have aged more, all of this attracted and repelled the child, who never stepped inside that tall house, but was content to inch open the padded front door sometimes, in idle hours, to catch with bated breath a rapid glimpse of the interior.

In a trunk in her bedroom were family papers, a few postcards from Dakar, Rio de Janeiro, Hong Kong, signed Charles or C. Liévens and addressed to Steenvoorde (North), France. The child of the high seas knew nothing about these faraway countries or about this Charles or this Steenvoorde.

She also kept a photo album, in a closet. One snapshot showed a child who very much resembled the little girl of the Ocean, and often the latter contemplated her with humility: it was always the image that seemed to be right, to be true; in one hand she held a hoop. The child had searched for one just like it in all the houses of the village. And one day she thought she'd found it: an iron circle from around a barrel. But hardly had she started running down the oceanic street with it than the hoop rolled out to sea.

In another photograph, the little girl could be seen between a man dressed in a sailor suit and a bony woman in her Sunday best. The child of the high seas, who'd never seen a man or woman, had wondered for a long time what these people wanted, wondered even in the depths of night, when lucidity can sometimes strike with a flash as violent as the lightning.

Every morning she went off to school, with a big briefcase stuffed full of notebooks, a grammar book, a book of arithmetic, a history of France, a geography book.

She also had a little treatise by Gaston Bonnier, Member of the Institute, Professor at the Sorbonne, and Georges de Layens, Laureat of the Academy of Sciences, which contained the most common plants, as well as the most useful and the most noxious plants, with eight hundred and nincty-cight diagrams.

She read the preface:

"Throughout the spring and summer months, nothing is easier than to pick large quantities of plants, in field and forest."

But history, geography, countries, great men, mountains, rivers and frontiers, how to explain it all to someone who knows only the empty street of a tiny village, in the deepest solitude of the Ocean. Even in the middle of the Ocean itself, the one portrayed in maps, she could not locate herself, although one day, for a second, she thought she had. But then she'd banished the idea as crazy and dangerous.

At a given moment, she sat and listened with absolute attention, wrote down several words, listened again, then went back to writing, as though an invisible schoolmistress were dictating a text to her. Then the child opened her grammar book and for a long time, her breath suspended, bent over page 60, exercise CLXVIII, of which she was particularly fond. There the grammar book seemed to speak, to address the little girl of the high seas directly:

> ____are you? ____are you thinking? ____are you speaking? ____do you want? ____should I address myself? ____is happening? ____do they accuse you? ____are you capable? ____are you culpable? ____is it about? ____did you get this gift? Eh! ____are you complaining?
> (Replace the spaces above with the correct interrogative pronoun, with or without the preposition.)

Sometimes the child felt an irresistible urge to write out certain sentences. And she did, with great precision.

Here are a few, from among many:

—Let's share this, okay?

—Listen to me closely. Sit down, don't move, I beg of you!

—If only a little snow fell from the high mountains, the day would go faster.

—Foam, foam around me, won't you at last turn into something hard?

—To dance in a circle, there have to be at least three of us.

—Two headless shadows were walking down the dusty road.

—Night, day, day, night, clouds and flying fish.

—I thought I heard a sound, but it was only the sound of the sea.

Or she wrote a letter in which she reported on her small town and herself. There was no salutation, and she didn't send her love to anyone at the end of the letter, and no name appeared on the envelope.

And when it was finished, she threw the letter into the sea—not to get rid of it, but because that's the way things had to be—perhaps like lost seafarers, who deliver their last message to the waves in a desperate bottle.

Time stood still in the floating village: the child was always twelve. And it did no good to stick out her chest in front of the wardrobe mirror in her bedroom. One day, tired of always looking like the photograph she kept in her album, with its braids and high forehead, she lost patience with herself and her portrait, and violently shook her hair out over her shoulders, hoping that would drastically change her age. Perhaps even the sea around her would undergo some metamorphosis and she would see great goats with foaming beards emerge from it, approaching her to take a look.

But the Ocean remained empty and the only visitors she had were shooting stars.

Another day there was a sort of lapse in destiny, a crack in its resolve. A real little freighter, smoking along, stubborn as a bulldog and riding the sea well, even though barely loaded (a beautiful red band stood out in the sun beneath the waterline), a freighter sailed down the watery village street, and the houses did not sink into the sea, nor the little girl into sleep.

It was high noon. The cargo ship sounded its foghorn, but its voice did not merge with the bell tower's. Each kept its singularity.

And hearing for the first time a sound that came to her from men, the child rushed to the window and shouted with all her might:

"Help!"

And she waved her schoolgirl apron in the ship's direction.

The helmsman didn't even turn his head. A sailor passed along the bridge blowing smoke rings, as though nothing were happening. Others did their laundry, while on each side of the bow the dolphins moved aside to make way for the speeding ship.

The little girl ran down to the street and lay in the freighter's wake, embracing it for so long that by the time she got up again, it was nothing more than a virginal patch of sea without any memory. Back inside the house, the child was stunned at having shouted, "Help!" Only then did she understand the deep meaning of the word. And that meaning terrified her. Hadn't the men heard her voice? Or were these sailors deaf and blind? Or crueler than the depths of the sea itself?

It was then that a wave came for her, which had always kept itself at some distance from the village, with visible reserve. This was an enormous wave, spreading side to side much farther than others. At the top it had two eyes of foam, two perfect imitations. You'd have thought it understood certain things and frowned on some of them. Even though it took shape and fell apart hundreds of times each day, it always came with these two well-defined eyes, always in the same place. At times, when something caught its interest, it could be seen, its crest suspended in the air for nearly a whole minute, forgetting it was a wave, which must begin again every seven seconds.

For a long time this wave had wanted to do something for the child, but hadn't known just what. Now it saw the cargo ship grow fainter in the distance and understood the anguish of the one who had been left behind. Unable to bear it any longer, the wave led the child not far from there, without a word, as if taking her by the hand.

After kneeling in front of her, as waves do, with the greatest respect, it rolled her to the bottom of itself and held her down a long long time, trying with death's collusion to remove her. And the little girl stopped breathing, to help the wave in its solemn project.

Not succeeding in its goal, it flung the child up in the air until she was no bigger than a sea bird, then caught her and flung her up again just like a ball, and she dropped back into foam flakes as big as ostrich eggs.

At last, seeing that there was nothing to be done, that it could never cause the child's death, the wave carried her home, with an immense murmur of tears and sorrow.

And the little girl, who didn't have one single scratch, was forced to open and close shutters hopelessly again, and disappear into the ocean temporarily, the moment a ship's mast pierced the horizon.

You sailors who dream at sea in the dark of night, your elbows resting on the railing of your ship, beware of thinking for too long of a beloved face. You risk giving birth, in a place which might as well be the desert, to a creature capable of every human feeling, who can neither live nor die nor love, yet suffers as though she were alive and felt love and was forever on the point of dying, a creature infinitely disinherited in the watery wastes, just like that child of the Ocean, born one day in the mind of Charles Liévens of Steenvoorde, deck hand on the four-master *The Bold,* who had lost his daughter, aged twelve, during one of his sea voyages, and one night, at latitude 55 degrees North, longitude 35 degrees West, thought about her with a terrible intensity, to the great misfortune of that child.

NK

Dramatic Sky at Montevideo Shore

LE SILLAGE

On voyait le sillage et nullement la barque
Parce que le bonheur avait passé par là!

Ils s'étaient regardés dans le fond de leurs yeux
Apercevant enfin la clairière attendue

Où courraient de grands cerfs dans toute leur franchise.
Les chasseurs n'entraient pas dans ce pays sans larmes.

Ce fut le lendemain, après une nuit froide,
Qu'on reconnut en eux des noyés par amour

Mais ce que l'on pouvait prendre pour leur douleur
Nous faisait signe à tous de ne pas croire en elle.

Un peu de leur voilure errait encore en l'air
Toute seule, prenant le vent pour son plaisir,

Loin de la barque et des rames à la dérive.

THE WAKE

We could see the wake but nothing of the boat
Because it was happiness that had passed by.

Looking at each other they had come at last
Deep within their eyes to the promised clearing

Where great stags were running at liberty,
No hunters visited this country without tears.

It was the next day after a night of cold
That they were recognized as drowned for love.

But what we might have taken for their grief
Assured us it was not to be trusted.

Part of their sail still floated in the air
Alone and free to take the wind as it pleased

Far from the boat and the oars drifting.

PT & KM

LE SURVIVANT

À Alfonso Reyes

Lorsque le noyé se réveille au fond des mers et que son coeur
Se met à battre comme le feuillage qui tremble
Il voit approcher de lui un cavalier qui marche à l'amble
Et qui respire à l'aise et lui fait signe de ne pas avoir peur.

Il lui frôle le visage d'une touffe de fleurs jaunes
Et se coupe devant lui une main sans qu'il y ait une goutte de rouge.
La main est tombée dans le sable où elle fond sans un soupir
Une autre main toute pareille a pris sa place et les doigts bougent.

Et le noyé s'étonne de pouvoir monter à cheval,
De tourner la tête à droite et à gauche comme s'il était au pays natal,
Comme s'il y avait alentour une grande plaine, la liberté,
Et la permission d'allonger la main pour cueillir un fruit de l'été.

Est-ce donc la mort cela, cette rôdeuse douceur
Qui s'en retourne vers nous par une obscure faveur?

Et serais-je noyé chevauchant parmi les algues
Qui voit comme se reforme le ciel tourmenté de fables.

Je tâte mon corps mouillé comme un témoignage faible
Et ma monture hennit pour m'assurer que c'est elle.

Un berceau bouge, l'on voit un pied d'enfant réveillé,
Je m'en vais sous un soleil qui semble frais inventé.

Alentour il est des gens qui me regardent à peine,
Visages comme sur terre, mais l'eau a lavé leurs peines.

Et voici venir à moi des paisibles environs
Les bêtes de mon enfance et de la Création

THE SURVIVOR

To Alfonso Reyes

When the drowned man awakens at the bottom of the sea and when his heart
Trembles like the leaves of an aspen tree
He sees coming toward him a man on a soft-gaited horse
Who breathes easily and whose gestures mean don't be afraid.

He touches the drowned man's face with a bunch of yellow flowers
And cuts off one of his own hands shedding no drop of blood.
The hand falls into the sand where it melts without a sigh
Another hand just like it takes its place and the fingers move.

And the drowned man is astonished to find he can ride a horse,
He can turn his head right and left just as if he were at home,
As if there were a broad plain all around him, freedom,
And permission to stretch out his hand to pick a summer fruit.

And is this death, this prowling gentleness
Which so strangely is kind enough to turn in our direction?

And this drowned man riding through seaweed – is it I myself
Who sees the sky changed by the torment of legends?

I touch my wet body as if to prove something,
And my mare neighs in case I was wondering if it were she.

A cradle moves, revealing the foot of an infant awakened.
I go my way in a sunlight that seems to be newly created.

Here and there are people who scarcely glance at me,
Their faces are as before, but with their sorrows washed away.

And now coming toward me from these tranquil surroundings
The animals of my childhood and of the Creation

Et le tigre me voit tigre, le serpent me voit serpent,
Chacun reconnaît en moi son frère, son revenant.

Et l'abeille me fait signe de m'envoler avec elle
Et le lièvre qu'il connaît un gîte au creux de la terre

Où l'on ne peut pas mourir.

The tiger sees me as a tiger, the snake as another snake,
Each recognizes in me his own brother, his ghost.

And the bee invites me to fly away with her,
And the hare knows a hiding place deep in the earth

Where no one ever dies.

PT & KM

LE REGRET DE LA TERRE

Un jour, quand nous dirons : "C'était le temps du soleil,
Vous souvenez-vous, il éclairait la moindre ramille,
Et aussi bien la femme âgée que la jeune fille étonnée,
Il savait donner leur couleur aux objets dès qu'il se posait.
Il suivait le cheval coureur et s'arrêtait avec lui,
C'était le temps inoubliable où nous étions sur la Terre,
Où cela faisait du bruit de faire tomber quelque chose,
Nous regardions alentour avec nos yeux connaisseurs,
Nos oreilles comprenaient toutes les nuances de l'air
Et lorsque le pas de l'ami s'avançait nous le savions,
Nous ramassions aussi bien une fleur qu'un caillou poli,
Le temps où nous ne pouvions attraper la fumée,
Ah ! c'est tout ce que nos mains sauraient saisir maintenant."

MISSING THE EARTH

Some day we will be saying, "That was the time of the sun,
Do you remember its light fell on the slightest twig,
The elderly woman or young astonished girl,
As soon as it touched, it gave their color to things
Kept pace with the galloping horse and stopped when he did,
That unforgettable time when we were still on Earth
Where if we dropped something it made a noise,
We would look around us with knowledgeable eyes,
And our ears distinguished every nuance in the air,
When the footsteps of a friend approached, we knew,
We used to gather flowers or smooth pebbles,
At that time we never could take hold of smoke,
Ah! What else can our hands do for us now?"

PT & KM

LA DEMEURE ENTOURÉE

Le corps de la montagne hésite à ma fenêtre:
"Comment peut-on entrer si l'on est la montagne,
Si l'on est en hauteur, avec roches, cailloux,
Un morceau de la Terre, altéré par le Ciel?"
Le feuillage des bois entoure ma maison:
"Les bois ont-ils leur mot à dire là-dedans?
Notre monde branchu, notre monde feuillu
Que peut-il dans la chambre où siège ce lit blanc,
Près de ce chandelier qui brûle par le haut,
Et devant cette fleur qui trempe dans un verre?
Que peut-il pour cet homme et son bras replié,
Cette main écrivant entre ces quatre murs?
Prenons avis de nos racines délicates,
Il ne nous a pas vus, il cherche au fond de lui
Des arbres différents qui comprennent sa langue."
Et la rivière dit: "Je ne veux rien savoir,
Je coule pour moi seule et j'ignore les hommes.
Je ne suis jamais là où l'on croit me trouver
Et vais me devançant, crainte de m'attarder.
Tant pis pour ces gens-là qui s'en vont sur leurs jambes.
Ils partent, et toujours reviennent sur leurs pas."
Mais l'étoile se dit: "Je tremble au bout d'un fil,
Si nul ne pense à moi je cesse d'exister."

THE HOUSE SURROUNDED

The mountain hesitates outside my window:
"How can I come in, if I am a mountain,
Extending, as I do, upwards, with rocks and pebbles,
A piece of the Earth, altered by the Sky?"
The foliage of woods surrounds my house:
"Have the woods nothing to say about all this?
Our world spread out in branches, our leafy world,
What can it do in that room with its white bed,
Where a candlestick is burning at its peak,
Close to that flower sipping from a glass?
What can it do for that man and his folded arm,
That hand writing in the shelter of four walls?
Let us take the opinion of our delicate roots,
He hasn't seen us, he searches within himself
For trees which understand what he has to say."
And the river: "This is no concern of mine;
I flow for myself alone and know nothing of men.
Wherever they find me, I have already gone,
Always ahead of myself, I'm afraid to linger.
Who cares about people who walk away on their legs?
They leave and always return the way they went."
But the star says, "Trembling, I hang by a thread,
I cease to exist if no one thinks of me."

PT & KM

On the trail through the center of the pampean desert, a man is proceeding, alone, on foot, carrying two bags slung over his shoulders and in one hand a suitcase. Despite the immensity of the landscape, which blurs his features a little, you can see he's of the Eastern type and must have left his country recently: sometimes he turns his head, as though followed. His determined little pipe surrounds him with an itinerant intimacy, its architecture unstable.

He has heard about a farm several leagues distant, and since morning he has been walking toward the blank horizon. At his feet, innumerable tracks on the road: he identifies the passage of sheep, oxen, horses, a desert of tracks, an unmoving world and the fruit of movement, filled with posthumous torpor.

Thus, from rancho to rancho, he has been traveling for several days. At night he sleeps where there is space to stretch out the body of a stranger who has spent the whole day walking. And when he lies awake, the birds charged with watching over the Earth's sleep—all kinds of owls, and others still, whose existence we will never know because they nest in the upper air—sound the hours for him with the Moon's consent.

On the San Tiburcio farm, where the man is headed, the ewes are being sheared in a shed. The creatures' eyes close under the cold breath of the shears, which rush impatiently the length of their woolly bellies, as though about to carry off, in passing, the delicate teats. One beast persists in sniffing at a shred of fleece that chance has placed beneath her muzzle. All the ewes' eyes seem to be made of glass, and interchangeable, like the anguish of their stressed bodies.

The itinerant Turk continues on his way. In the shadows of his belt it is five o'clock, according to his nickel watch, warm with the journey, but it's much later in his mind: he hurries, as if he's been awaited for some time and a chair has already been placed for him, in the middle of the room.

The shearing continues in the shed at San Tiburcio.

Juan Pecho, that man crouching over to your left, must be the boss. The knife in his belt, beneath the vest that lifts as he works, is longer than those of the peons. Tall, fat, he shears ponderously: everywhere in his body an enormous indolence lounges, confiding in him, even as he makes a show of working. In place as soon as he wakes up, it leaves him only at night, to take a little stroll while he is sleeping and no longer really needs it. The discolored cigarette butt on his lower lip seems to have been stuck there for five or six years.

He shears badly and distractedly. From time to time insults go astray in the hairs of his sparse beard.

The ewes who have to deal with him do not forget the heavy shadow cast by this body leaning over them, these gashes, this ox breath. He would rather slit their throats. It's quicker, and isn't blood the only distraction in the pampa for a gaucho faithful to his fiancée?

The dogs' first barks come to lodge in the Turk's ear. Until then, for hours on end, he's been a man only to the wind sweeping the pampa, and an odd man, at that, since he is traveling on foot in a land where everyone rides horseback. Juan Pecho and the children have seen him. They ascribe to him a country, emotions, a character.

He's the peddler of baubles and trinkets, whose very boxes people love. All over the world, men, women, children love these boxes. The planet needs them, as one of the places where destiny takes shape, hides, schemes.

This opportunity is not to be passed up by Juan Pecho, who stands and mounts the horse always saddled near him, not for fear of keeping the future waiting, but because never in his life has he walked fifteen feet in a row.

Rolling a cigarette, he heads for the stranger.

"*Buenas tardes,* do you wish to see the merchandise of a passing tradesman who is at your service?" the Turk makes an attempt to say in Spanish. "Here in the Argentinian Republic I represent several large foreign firms."

"You represent?" says the farmer, with a nasty smile, looking pointedly at the man's bags.

The Turk lowers his eyes, caught in his lie. Hunger and the wide open spaces have made him inventive.

"Follow me," says Pecho, turning his back.

He debates whether to take the stranger to the shearing shed or the kitchen. The presence of his sister Florisbela, grave and wide, at the rancho's gate, decides him.

"Here's a Turk who's going to spend the night. We'll see what he's brought after dinner. Between then and now, no displaying his wares."

Then under his breath:

"Watch out, he's got long fingers."

The peddler asks Florisbela for water and disappears behind some weeds.

He returns washed, brushed, perfumed, and sits down on a stool facing the sunset, not far from Florisbela who is drinking maté.

Neither says a word, intimidated by the falling night. Stars still dazzled by the light of day look blindly on. The ewes whom the work of shearing has separated from their lambs search for them in the folds of twilight, and from earth to sky all is but one unbroken bleating, pricked with stars and fireflies.

The Turk was beginning to feel his weariness. A thought, a stray arrow—shot by whom?—crossed his mind. And he checked to make sure his revolver was in his pocket. Just then, Juan Pecho's voice could be heard. He was coming toward the rancho, followed by Florisbela's three children, the oldest of whom, Horacio, had the face at twelve of a grown man and limped badly. Dogs encircled the little group.

"No, no!" the farmer was saying absently, in a low voice. "Not until after dinner! The Turk will set up his things on the table and we'll have plenty of time to look."

Florisbela concurred. As the peddler would have liked to do immediately. But not understanding Spanish very well, he didn't comprehend the phrase till seconds later, after having struggled with the words, in secret, deep inside his ear.

Everyone entered the huge room that served as both kitchen and diningroom.

"Here," said Juan Pecho to the stranger, assigning him a place in the corner.

One by one, the estancia's eight mongrels came to smell the intruder and attempted to lift their hind legs on his luggage. But he stopped them with deferential gestures.

Inside the rancho people spoke with lowered voices; Florisbela and her old father, a white-bearded gaucho with an extraordinarily distinguished air, wanted to permit the Turk to sit at the familial table, and the children all whispered: "Yes, yes, yes, yes!"

"He eats in the corner, on his knees," breathed Juan Pecho violently.

And he thought: *It's bad enough I've let him in my house—this* gringo, *this itinerant who's still on earth by luck alone, this ghost who just to play the big shot asks for water the minute he arrives, so he can clean up. He even washed his feet out in the open, as if you don't need to keep such things to yourself.*

From the shed, Juan Pecho had followed the Turk's movements and seen his red-striped towel as he was drying himself in the last rays of the sun.

When the meat was cooked, the farmer and his family sat down at table, in the corner the Turk, with his clean feet, bony and sad. (If the face is obliged to smile for professional purposes, our human sadness must take refuge elsewhere.)

Beneath the odor of roasted meat, the stranger admitted to himself he liked his nomadic life, and in the same moment remembered his name, Ali ben Salem, and his love of parents and country, along with other less precise virtues and the essential facts of his biography.

The weariness of his legs and back, which was beginning to seem ideal, kept him company.

At the table over which Juan Pecho presided, everyone wanted to appear sure of their roof and a tomorrow, because of the vagabond's presence. They used their forks ostentatiously, since he had only a knife and cut his meat level with his mouth. From where they sat, Florisbela's children couldn't take their eyes off the Turk's jaws.

After dinner and the five minutes of silence that followed it, Juan Pecho, who didn't want to seem overeager, said at last: "Let's see."

The children rushed to get the peons and soon, along with them, around the riches of the peddler were gathered Florisbela's old father, she herself and Juan Pecho, all standing immobile, as austere as the desert.

On the table, in little cardboard boxes, credulous golden metal (brooches, bracelets, earrings, lucky charms) smiled at the same time as Ali ben Salem's lips and in connivance with them. The mineral concentration of the spectators, becoming human at last, gave way to several gestures.

This gold moved slowly into them, lining their souls. To right and left were spread all kinds of objects for grooming, haberdashery and perfumery, in brand-new colors, forming a sort of motley urban springtime on the table.

"Feel free to touch," said the Turk.

Then the brown hands of the peasants could be seen advancing like carp around a piece of bread.

Juan Pecho was saying nothing yet, although quick glances often flickered toward him.

While his beard rounded his face more nonchalantly than ever, he opened a box that held a safety razor and, in the general silence, asked how it worked. He thought how much it mattered to him to show up close-shaven the next Sunday, at the house of Esther Llanos, his betrothed.

"How much for the razor?"

"Three little piastres. It's like silk."

"Three piastres! I'll give you one," said Pecho, in a rough voice.

Filled with gentleness, the Turk repeated: "I can't, I can't," through a hundred smiles that canceled one another out, and who knows if beneath his shirt his shaggy chest wasn't feeling amiable too, in its way.

His gaze locked on the razor, the farmer was thinking: "Three piastres, the price of a sheep with all his wool for this scrap of shiny metal!" Meanwhile Florisbela, the old man, the peons were buying things and silver coins were seen to change pockets in the unflinching lamplight.

Juan Pecho's mute rage began to poison the air.

The peons moved away from the room. Seated on their pallets, they waited.

The Turk wrapped up his things, except for the razor, which he felt escaping him in response to the farmer's violent desire.

The old man, who hadn't said a word, the woman, the children, all of them in a fatal immobility.

"Why are you looking at me!" burst from the master.

The sound of scraping chairs. Faces became backs, disappearing one by one, through the open door into the dark of night.

Now there remains nothing in the room except Juan Pecho, the razor and the Turk.

The Creole wonders if he isn't going to dismiss the peddler, but then he'd have to offer reasons, or at least to put two words together… He decides it's more convenient to step back a pace and plant his knife in the neck located right in front of him.

The Turk falls headfirst, arms outstretched as if he didn't want to hurt himself, and slumps abruptly into death.

A dog enters, a night spirit, charged with a mission; he smells the body, notes the death and leaves, crushing his own shadow.

Pecho seizes the razor and, opening the suitcase, picks up some soap, then closes the door and puts out the lamp to obliterate the traces of blood. In the room next door he carefully shaves, astonishing himself with this new face the mirror shapes, as if it were a long-lost relative who has just crossed the seas. From time to time, he turns back toward the door, behind which the corpse is already making arrangements for its immobile trip. When he is finished, he approaches the body. Its unbuttoned jacket exposes a wide belt of new leather. Suddenly Juan Pecho knits his brows: it is his duty to examine the belt's contents. Its buckle undone, the sound of gold rings out indistinctly, like an alarm clock hardly muffled under blankets. On the table Pecho counts twenty pounds sterling. This presence deeply displeases him: he did not kill for this, he's not a thief. The various objects in the Turk's bags do not count: an amusement for the eyes and hands, of superficial use.

He does not want these coins, these intermediaries between the deceased and unknown strangers, who are perhaps starting to wonder, in the night, to move in their beds, light the lamp, look at the hour, understand that somewhere in the world something grave is taking place and they must go and find out just what's happening.

An idea occurs to him: with this gold he will do a good deed.

One by one, he slides the pounds sterling into his lame nephew's piggy bank. The purified gold now flows on the side of the angels.

In the Turk's pocket he leaves the money paid by Florisbela and the peons for their purchases. His conscience clear, he considers the suitcases and bags with gloomy sympathy. Then he empties them out on the table, and makes several piles.

"For my very dear sister Florisbela," he writes on a scrap of paper, in his awkward handwriting.

"For the mischievous Mariquita."

"For my little nephew Juan Albertito."

"For my esteemed father."

"For Juan Pecho."

A long leather strap attached around the Turk's neck and here's Pecho on horseback riding through the chaste night, which steps back as he passes. He is going to throw the body in the pond, close by. Two wild ducks fly up toward the Southern Cross.

He hasn't forgotten the stone tied to the neck. Juan Pecho returns to the rancho. From sleep, into which he plunges instantly, he's not awakened until dawn by the birds who peck at his last nightmare.

Freezing cold, as though he had slept underwater, he watches the sun rise over the pond and tries to convince himself that the Turk drowned there.

So I divided his things up between us, rather than throwing them in the water where no one would have benefited from them.

And I was absolutely right.

Florisbela had heard the body fall. On the rancho's bloodstained floor she threw a little of the earth that had spent the night beneath the sky. Then, her back turned, she began to pray.

Slowly, Juan Pecho's surprise grew as he saw no peons heading for the shed. Without even claiming their pay for the shearing, all three of them had left before dawn.

Four days later, Florisbela approached her brother and murmured in his ear: "He's floating."

The man leapt up as though he had to kill the Turk a second time.

His stomach enormous, his head thrown back, pretentious and livid, the Turk was floating.

Another bigger stone around the neck and, most important, the stomach slashed because of the gases, and the Oriental left again for invisible adventures.

It was on returning to the ranch that for the first time since his crime Pecho noticed toothbrushes, combs, hairpins, soap, cloth, thimbles, jewelry, tins of shoe polish scattered on the ground.

"Pick all that up," he shouted at his nephews. "You little murderers!'

"Go see if he's floating," said Horatio to Mariquita.

"It's your turn."

"I just went. Now you go."

They'd had to set up visiting hours at the pond. Eight days went by without Ali ben Salem's bursting to the surface of the globe again.

On the ninth, two mounted policemen presented themselves at the rancho's gate. Their identical mission lent them a horrible resemblance to each other; calm and thin, their drooping mustaches looked false.

"Let's go, my friend," said the sergeant who was holding the handcuffs.

Passing the pond in the commissioner's wagon, Juan Pecho saw that the Turk hadn't floated to the surface. Then how did the police...? The denunciation had certainly not come from the peons, who were too proud to turn in a man for whom they'd worked, nor had it come from Florisbela, nor the others who lived at the rancho.

And when the commissioner asked the Creole if anyone had seen the crime committed, he suddenly remembered: "Yes, Señor, a dog."

NK

THE ESTANCIA

Our mounts were waiting for us on the opposite bank. Then, between our family and us, there was the dust stirred by our horses on a lengthy trail, a river six hundred meters wide, and the certainty that we would not be going back for thirty-six hours. To be able to look gauchos in the eye, to be high up on galloping beasts, to make them go forward, wheel round ten times, twenty times if we felt like it—this was a joy made all the more intense for us because no one had taught us how to ride a horse. Just as little black children in Dakar aren't taught to swim or newborns in the four corners of the world to cry. Déhère showed us how to saddle our horses, how to slip the bit between their teeth without disturbing the tongue, how to place the recado and lambskins with the greatest care, how to fasten it all. And there were our horses, ready beneath our hands, coming and going before our eyes. We ourselves were making reality, and then we were touching this reality, huge, beautiful, alive. We became familiar with its volume, weight, consistency. The lesson of things, of things. It was in the Uruguayan countryside that I felt for the first time I was touching the things of this world, and racing along behind them!

At a gallop, we drove the cows toward barbed wire fences, and forced them to turn, to pivot on their own panic. Suddenly face to face with bewildered cattle. Cows of my childhood, yes, it's you I'm talking about. Cows scattered across the countryside, like the words of some incomprehensible communication, always scrambled, what difficult things you had to tell us, with your muffles, your snuffling, your ridiculous tails, continuously seeking equilibrium for your whole body, what things in those black eyes, crosscut with anguished white, in that hot and panting meat, steered by horned heads, so much roughness, crudeness, gossiping and schemes, what things, you vagabonds of the plain! And how we wanted to caress you, to rub your muzzles, to brush you, kick you, understand you, grave beasts, dear, hot and stupid, oh you, laughingstock, your udders constantly emptied by calves as big as you!

Best of all the animals in the world (I say this as though you hadn't already noticed) I love the cow of the pampas—skinny, bastard, stray—who so little resembles Victor Hugo's:

Superb, enormous, mottled red and white
Sweet as a doe with tender fawns
Beautifully grouped beneath her belly.

Because emotion causes bovines to lose weight, chasing cows was a forbidden joy. Déhère did not allow us to upset them. And often I was forced to admire them quietly, at a distance. They lent the countryside strange nuances, absurd and touching. Sometimes, for me who already knew France, they took the place in the deserted Uruguayan landscape of a peasant in his cart bound for the fair, sometimes of a town stilled beneath the heat of day, a laborer and his plough, men playing *boules* or drinking in the doorway of an inn! They carried all the landscape's weight, all the responsibility.

I think of the handful of Spanish cows, the single bull, the few horses that came ashore in the 16th century in the province of Buenos Aires, to whom the republics of the Rio de la Plata owe a great part of their wealth.

There was a time (from 1650 to 1720) when those I wouldn't want to name again were mistresses of Uruguay. They were seen grazing in groups of twenty, fifty, a thousand, heroic beasts at the mercy of wild animals, epidemics, drought, torrential rains. In this country as empty of fences as the country of the Moon, they moved often, happy for a change of air, and curious about new pastures. And birds came fluttering to wish them welcome by alighting on the tips of their horns.

The settlers back then scarcely dared to leave the coast, and you found in the interior only scattered Indians, generally drunk, dressed in a few ostrich feathers. They lived on good terms with the cattle, especially by flattering them with crudeness—I mean by rolling joyfully in fresh cow dung. This, along with war, was their favorite pastime.

It was truly the cows, horses, sheep "who carried out the conquest of the provinces of the Rio de la Plata. They accomplished what neither Juan Diaz de Solis nor, later, Gaboto Martinez de Irala and Juan Ortiz de Zarate could, with their military expeditions: to settle these territories securely. In the course of one hundred and twenty-five years, the few bovines introduced into Uruguay had become an immense herd: twenty-five million head."[*]

---

[*]Supervielle's note: *Book for the Centenary of Independence (1825–1925),* published in Montevideo under the direction of M. Perfecto Lopez Campana.

The government of Buenos Aires authorized the "faeneros" to hunt beasts with horns "in return for a fee of one-third." Uruguay, then called "Banda Oriental," constituted a huge cattle ranch for Buenos Aires. Well-armed expeditions traveled upriver in boats.

The hunters were divided into two teams. One of them consisted of men on horseback, furnished with long lances that ended in steel crescents. Top speed, emitting cries and curses, they flung themselves at the poor gallop-on-a-zigzag creatures, whose Achilles tendons they sliced through. The other team finished off the beasts, amid a great lowing, and the cawing of crows and eagles, and the barking of stray dogs. Each ate his favorite morsel, then they abandoned all the rest, meat having no value. The hides, the tallow and the grease were sent to Buenos Aires. It was important that the hunters keep their eyes on their mounts, always in danger of being lured away and swept off into the interior by wild horses.

On the Uruguayan coast, especially in the region of Maldonado, pirates set up shop. One of them, Étienne Moreau, a Frenchman, became famous. He and his men slaughtered a considerable number of cows and exported their hides. To defend himself against attacks by the Spanish authorities, Moreau succeeded in disembarking artillery, seriously fortifying his warehouses.

It was, in Uruguay, "the leather age." Whole ranchos were constructed of leather: doors, beds, chests, baskets, cradles. Carts were covered with it, it was used to cross rivers. (What a pungency of leather from one end of Uruguay to the other!) And an excellent method of torturing thieves and bandits was to put them in vests of still-warm hide and expose them to the hot sun.

Land of red meat, land where veal is never eaten! From early morning on, we were in contact with the cows; they were in charge of waking us, in the shape of a rare *churrasco,* which we ate in the kitchen, rubbing from our eyes the remainder of sleep and the smoke of "home." Land of milk fresh from the cow, which we drank so close to the cattle that their flies became ours, sometimes to the point of being in our milk. Beautiful Saturdays, when we simply could not manage to go to bed. Sundays when we thought they'd never wake us early enough to gallop off into the wide open spaces.

Déhère's wife seemed palpably older than he. I can still see her in her kitchen, eyes lit by the embers, as she wipes her hands on her apron, amid the scent of grilled meat. I think also of her dark pretty daughters whom I loved to watch. But what's the good of these confidences. Uruguay, why call forth confessions that no one asks of me? They're of interest only to an eight-year-old child with whom I cannot even go for a short ride in the country, a child I've lost all hope of meeting. How I wish that I could one day ask him for the time, then hurry off, not mentioning my name, or his!

After dinner we played *mus* with Déhère and his daughters. A Basque game, "spoken." Spanish cards.

"Envido."

"Quiero."

"Hordago!"

What happiness to measure ourselves on equal terms against the man who provided us with horses. And our hands just as proud to hold our cards as they had been earlier to hold the reins of our mounts. In the city we were no more than children; here, the boss's children, happy and a little overawed behind the dry beans that we used to keep track of points and victory.

Déhère took the trouble to name for us the birds, insects, plants, trees of the country, and we thought them the exclusive property of Uruguay (well, perhaps they might be found in the Argentinian Republic, but nowhere else!). Thus, teru-teros, in their black and white flight, their cries sharp—*teru-tero!*—proud and tenacious, keeping watch like guard dogs around the houses, as around their nests, whose eggs were so sought-after; "the only birds who lead the way into danger," say Uruguayan naturalists, birds who are so much a part of the national patrimony that they're found even on the country's postage stamps.

How to admit now that the teru-tero is none other than the plover? But is it really altogether the same bird? I do hope not, and hope that one day somebody will prove it.

We also had on the estancia pink ibis and herons like those in Egypt, and capybaras like those in Brasil. Capybara: "Giant rodent, with grooved upper incisors, diving under water at the first sign of danger, and living in mud like tapirs." The timid armadillo with the delicately downy carapace, pleasant to the touch, which you cook like a suckling pig. The partridge, the snipe, the wild duck. The iguana, that large lizard, fast as a greyhound, lurking around the fowls whose eggs it eats, first breaking the shell with its tail. And a few snakes, here and there, when you least expected it, like *memento mori*.

Sometimes, as we were returning to the estancia, after long gallops in the countryside, I heard the chaja's strident cry. It stopped me in my tracks, to warn me of I knew not what. Bird of repentance, of self-reflection, in my mouth you called forth the sad taste of blood. Where do you get this power, heavy bird who has such difficulty lifting into flight (on what insects, worms, fish larvae do you nourish yourself? where do you dip your wading-bird talons?); where do you get this power to penetrate us so abruptly and with your terrible short cries to call everything into question in the hearts of children and men, bird heard for a league around, you who pronounce your name so clearly: chaja! You were the first to ask me what I was doing on the earth and just where I thought I was going in the sandy pampas, brown long-necked bird, on your high talons and your wings armed with two spurs in the front, chaja the screamer, *chaouna torquata*.

On the estancia animals lived and died in front of us. The city hides its dead and wounded. The [South] American countryside makes you witness all the pangs of death. Here, bones spring up as numerous as thorns and thistles. I promised myself not to talk to you about death, but here we are in the open country, and how could I hide from you these horses, these sheep, these cows lying on their sides, their eyes a metallic black and blue, their eyes already reflecting tomorrow's fat flies, their necks so desperately stretched forward, as if salvation were there, so close, a few centimeters away, and they were dying solely because their necks had not stretched out just a little farther.

But let me think of those other beasts, more beautiful in Uruguay than anywhere else, who do not die, not they. You see them disappear, that's all, and without suffering, before your very eyes. Their shapes are unstable, always restless, but so soft to caress (I'd like to say, if that were not pure folly). The clouds! And those only a country with little rain can offer, slow clouds, grave and well-constructed, shaped with the greatest care, splendid storms, composed with an extraordinary sense of drama, storms in several acts, fully expecting applause. Storms sometimes dry, featuring thunder and lightning just for the pleasure of it. Clouds with sumptuous breasts, with sterile wombs. And you would need to travel to the south of France, near Avignon, to find such light, at one and the same time infinite and meticulous, neglecting nothing.

The day of our first arrival at the estancia we'd thought we were on one enormous plain, unvarying, all of a piece. But with experience we distinguished two quite different parts, one low and swampy, near the river, from which it was separated by a cloud of reeds, the other rich in pasturage and thistles.

Not far from the river grew a thorny wood, formed of *talas* and *espinillos,* their leaves like the tips of arrows. We hoped someday to find Indians there. Several *ceibos* too, with red flowers having the shape, consistency and plumpness of lovely sensual lips.

We tied up our horses and walked between the brambles into a veritable scrubland, looking for those men who, fifty years before, had lost all hope of surviving here. Sometimes we met a stray sheep who seemed to wander out of the depths of time. This makes me think of those who roamed without a master at the beginning of the 18th century and often 'fell prey to wild dogs. Toward 1730, the government of Montevideo ordered every head of family living in the countryside to kill two dogs per month. They submitted to the mayor, against a receipt, four dog ears. You had to pay a réal for a missing ear. And this is in part why today Uruguay has eighteen million sheep and consents to lose a few of them deep in the woods.

In the eucalyptus bordering the house, when our games grew quiet, we heard a chattering and a great jumble of wings and beaks. I paid only vague attention, even though sometimes this was the very noise that woke me, mornings. How amazed I was to observe, on one of my trips fifteen years later, that these noisy birds with their staccato flight were completely green, of a beautiful shiny green, sure of itself. I was so distracted that it took me five crossings of the Atlantic at its widest point (or almost) to realize that the estancia, where I had spent so many days, abounded in parakeets. Uruguay, the Uruguay of my childhood, was far less distant than I'd thought from the Tropic of Capricorn, in the hot regions of the Earth.

During summer vacation, we loved to go into a neighboring property to gallop across fields of grass and brambles. Grass, we said, to simplify things; but how many different grasses, how many forest flowers we crushed: goat's beard, virgin hair, air carnations, horsetails, devil's horns and nails, little bird flowers, little duck flowers, toad flowers, flowers of the angelus, rooster eggs, dog tears, cow tongues, bull's blood, peasant-girl sighs, monk tripe, little partridge grass. And all those still awaiting names beneath our horses' hooves. After three or four leagues, we arrived at an estancia that was much more primitive than ours, and which in its three thousand hectares possessed one single tree, an ombu. In Uruguay, the ombu, like the teru-tero, has an almost national importance. They might have put its image, too, on postage stamps. It is a solemn tree, often enormous, with partially visible roots: there are few in the world who possess such meaning and importance. It grows in solitude, as if to the plains it were no more than an intense desire for wood, for foliage, painfully embodied. And it's a very busy tree. All by itself, it must offer shade to men, as well as dogs and horses, saddled or not, who sometimes wait there, hours on end, with the patience of bones beneath the earth. It must also allow great big nails to be hammered into it, from which quarters of meat are hung. And when a child dies, on distant estancias, its little coffin is still placed on a high branch of the tree. In order that the soul not have too hard a time departing, the cover remains raised all night long.

Although of imposing appearance, the ombu is not terribly robust: must we admit that the most beautiful indigenous tree of Uruguay is made of spongy wood, its trunk hollow, and that it belongs to a family of herbaceous plants! It is a kind of monstrous grass, a mere attempt at a tree, but it holds the soil admirably, and I never saw any uprooted.

The ombu that I loved to contemplate on the neighboring estancia had been completely stripped on its south side by the *pampero*. It bore to the north all of its energy, and its compact foliation. In its struggle with the wind it had literally tamped itself down, concentrated itself, and although it had the corpulence of handsome trees in every country, it displayed the deformity, the contortions, and the puny malice of a bonsai tree from Japan. (To resist the wind, our horses did the opposite of the ombu; they turned toward it a powerful rump, where the bulk of their strength seemed concentrated.)

After dinner Déhère liked to tell us stories, to explain working in the fields to us. Sometimes, between two tales, a nocturnal mooing or the shrill voice of a ewe traversed the diningroom and moved on. To make his meaning clear, the Basque believed in using everything that came to hand and, when needed, he took from his pockets a knife, a piece of string.

"Supposition…," he would begin. "This—" (he placed a table knife in front of him) "is a herd of sheep, not yet sheared. I want to drive them over here. Supposition—" (he advanced his soup spoon) "here's a ewe who's being sheared…"

In the diningroom we made as many suppositions as he wished. There were also stories about gauchos, revolutions. But I don't remember them, and before going my way, I'd like to take leave of this Déhère, our supplier of horses, horizons, lovely tales. I'd like to say how angry I was at you, Déhère, to learn some years ago that you were nothing but a hypocrite, wanting to please the children of a boss whom you were cheating, and so hard on those who worked under your orders that none dared to denounce you. Long-gone Déhère, how to take back all the admiration in our childish eyes, the violent affection with which we encircled you, you who were betraying us with such a sure hand, you whose eyes so sparkled with true goodness, generosity, devotion, you scoundrel!

NK

GAUCHOS

Here's a gaucho who has come to Montevideo on his piebald horse, a little too showy. The gaucho likes to go noticed. Silver spurs, silver appliqués on saddle and bridle. And a look announcing he needs nothing and no one. He will not deign to see a single passerby and proceeds down the crowded street as if he were in the open countryside.

And yet how deeply he desires to stop before saddleries and pastry shops! But let's not meddle with his private business. We are embarrassed to see clearly into his heart.

Do we in fact see so clearly?

Tramways, tramways, leave him be! You too, hackney cabs and private carriages, carts from the port! And you, passersby, civilized men, stop staring at this gaucho. He's sensitive, more so than many of you. It's he who should intimidate you: the pampas ride with him and isolate him in the middle of the crowd.

At the end of an hour beneath these gimlet-eyed stares, he's had enough of being here and turns to go home at a little trot, the thirty piastres he came to spend unspent; he returns to his desert as if he longed to enter the kingdom of his solitary heart.

When a gaucho bothers to speak in your presence, listen to him. It is always pertinent, even if the words are pronounced in a calm and unemphatic way. As if a stone had started speaking.

Example: a Frenchman is vacationing on an estancia. (This was during the last revolution, more than twenty years ago.) He advances in a tilbury drawn by a very handsome anglo-arab, recently imported. A horseman precedes him, a peasant. The hunting has been good: several teal, two wild ducks, a partridge. The hunter is hungry. As he takes the shortest way home:

"*Es mejor por aqui* (This way is better)," says the peasant, indicating a path which requires a slight detour.

The foreigner really doesn't see why he should lengthen his trip and, without responding, he takes his usual route as though he hadn't heard.

Three hundred meters farther on, as he is leaving a little wood of espinillos, marauders shoot him at point-blank range. He hasn't even time to defend himself. The peasant too is struck down, one leg broken. They take his horse and the one pulling the tilbury, which they hastily unhitch. The Frenchman is shot through the stomach, with a bullet in his head, and just enough time to ask the gaucho:

"Rodriguez my friend, why on earth didn't you warn me this road wasn't safe…"

"I told the gentleman: *Es mejor por aqui.*"

The gaucho is proud and never shows his astonishment. One of my friends brought a phonograph to a very distant estancia where nothing like it had ever been seen before.

Somewhere between an ombu tree and a ranch house, in front of three dogs and four gauchos, the phonograph has its say.

My friend asks one of the peasants for his impression.

"*Regular* (Not bad)," answers the man.

And in the same instant another gaucho can be seen answering the call of nature against the ombu.

Hipolito Hernandez left the pampas for the first time in his life to travel to a neighboring town, six leagues from his home, where there lived one of his sisters, Maria, recently married.

It's morning. The gaucho has gone out on the balcony. The woman leaves to get bread from the baker, crosses the street (or rather the path), after having covered her head with a napkin to protect herself from the already harsh sun. She returns to prepare lunch. Hernandez is still on his balcony, smoking, taking some maté. After half an hour a man comes walking down the village street.

"Hey, Maria, here's someone to see you," says the gaucho, for whom any passerby must be a visitor.

The sister looks into the street and doesn't say anything. And the man outside continues on his way. And the gaucho serves himself a new maté. It's lunchtime. After the puchero, they offer Hernandez olives. He attempts to spear one with his fork and doesn't succeed. His sister does, on her first try.

"It's not surprising," says Hipolito. "The olive was worn-out."

"You want some cheese?"

"No, cheese is *traicionero* (treacherous)."

"Milk?"

"Yes, milk is an *instrument* we use at home."

"Would you like an orange?"

"No, the orange is very unfriendly."

After lunch the woman asks her brother:

"Do you play dominos?"

"No, it's a difficult game," says the gaucho, solemnly. "You'd have to know the grammar."

At twilight he leaves his sister to go back to the estancia.

"Aren't you afraid of ghosts?" asks the woman.

"No, I'm *accompanied* (I am carrying a talisman)."

And there goes Hipolito Hernandez, returning home, very straight in his saddle, at his mount's little trot, the tiny little trot that permits him to cover so many leagues.

Next day, at dawn, he goes looking for horses on the plain. He corrals some twenty of them—and two mules—into the paddock. Why the two mules, which haven't been used for several years? Who knows. In the pampa, suddenly, here's the inexplicable. And, this time, the inexplicable is looking you straight in the eye; it has two very long ears, and they're twitching.

The horses stand there, indifferent, their necks horizontal, sometimes waiting for hours at a time to be needed, blinking their eyes in an immobile stupor. They seem to be sleeping, more or less, under the sweetness of the lukewarm sun, which gilds their hairy discolored hide. Fatigue, sparse grass, burning heat and naked winters, drought, and rains that beat on their backs, everything has marked their furrowed bodies: they seem to wait for death, in a corner of the large enclosure, pressed up against each other, like a raft in the middle of the sea.

And yet at the first summons they will embark, full of docile courage, on interminable rides, as tough as their thin, glum, marvelous riders.

The gaucho rarely drinks alcohol; he substitutes maté. Many are the virtues of this green infusion, green and bitter, which the man of the fields generally drinks without sugar from a gourd, through a metal straw.

Strange maté, which insinuates itself throughout the body, always up to its old tricks: diuretic, laxative, it excites the brain and slows the heartbeat. It replaces the vegetables the gaucho does not cultivate (he is no gardener). Maté allows him to live exclusively on meat.

And it stimulates! It takes hold of the very soul of man and establishes itself there. Thanks to its influence, the man from before the maté, the humble man of just a minute ago, bone-tired, extinguished, seems to have become a stranger.

The gaucho moves from violent act to pure dream with the greatest of ease. Like poets and children he has no need of sleep to be precipitated into dreaming. He chews up space, in such strong doses that it takes the place, for him, of hashish. What an expression in his eyes, around his mouth, because of everything he wishes he could say better, he who thinks awkwardly and disposes of only a few hundred words, almost always pronounced in a monotonous voice… One day I saw emerging from some ranchos several peasants, their wives, their children, all coming to meet certain among us. Big and little, in a line, they extended a hardened hand, which they leaned against ours without grasping it, saying in one breath, as though it were a single word:

"*Como-le-va-bien-y-Usted. Como-le-va-bien-y-Usted.* (How-are-you-fine-and-you.)"

In joy as in anger, each time his heart leaps the man of the pampas thinks of his knife. It really helps him to express himself. Scarcely a few years ago, you often saw two gauchos, old friends, bumping into one another unexpectedly after a long separation, who drew their only weapons in sign of delight, and with their ponchos half-rolled around their left arms for shields, played at who would be the first to cause the other's blood to spurt.

"Old Rodriguez, here he is!"

"Damned Montes, always the same!"

Montes parries left and aims at his friend's right shoulder. The blow is avoided.

"So how's the health, always good?"

"As you see," says Montes, trying to wound his comrade on the leg to make him limp, just for fun.

"And what have you been doing all this time?"

"As you see, as you see…"

And the dueling with knives continues until, after an abrupt hand-to-hand:

"Damn it, Rodriguez," says Montes. "No, you're joking, come on now…"

And Montes tears up his poncho to dress the wound. We will never know if it's fatal or not: Montes's back, bent over his dear fallen friend, his enormous back is blocking our view, even if we bend our heads to right or left as much as possible.

The gaucho's vitality is unfathomable. One of them is dying from a knife wound in the chest. The priest, after Extreme Unction, asks is there anything else he can offer.

"A *churrasco* (a beefsteak)," says the dying man, his eyes already glassy.

And there he is: he eats and revives.

Simple gauchos, solemn and sensitive, in you the feeling of grandeur is so natural that in order never to forget it we need only once see you come to our door, at the end of the day, to "inquire about tomorrow's orders." You suddenly awaken distances and skies inside our narrow houses, and in your presence the ceiling seems about to light up slowly and majestically with stars, the ceiling which in your land is called *sleek sky.*

But your kind is disappearing, and several times I've heard it said: "Gauchos? There *are* no more of them!" It's true that they have lost their wild look. Railroads, highways, education. Isn't there even, in Uruguay, "a traveling agronomy professorship," complete with museum, lecture hall in a special coach, and consultation room for estancieros and simple peasants, who show up at the nearest railway station for the news, the very latest news of science and progress…

NK

Gaucho Festival, Uruguay

À LAUTRÉAMONT

N'importe où je me mettais à creuser le sol espérant que tu en sortirais
J'écartais du coude les maisons et les forêts pour voir derrière.
J'étais capable de rester toute une nuit à t'attendre, portes et fenêtres ou-
    vertes
En face de deux verres d'alcool auxquels je ne voulais pas toucher.
Mais tu ne venais pas,
Lautréamont.

Autour de moi des vaches mouraient de faim devant des précipices
Et tournaient obstinément le dos aux plus herbeuses prairies,
Les agneaux regagnaient en silence le ventre de leurs mères qui en
    mouraient,
Les chiens désertaient l'Amérique en regardant derrière eux
Parce qu'ils auraient voulu parler avant de partir.
Resté seul sur le continent
Je te cherchais dans le sommeil où les rencontres sont plus faciles.
On se poste au coin d'une rue, l'autre arrive rapidement
Mais tu ne venais même pas,
Lautréamont,
Derrière mes yeux fermés.
Je te rencontrais un jour à la hauteur de Fernando Noronha
Tu avais la forme d'une vague mais en plus véridique, en plus
    circonspect,
Tu filais vers l'Uruguay à petites journées.
Les autres vagues s'écartaient pour mieux saluer tes malheurs,
Elles qui ne vivent que douze secondes et ne marchent qu'à la mort
Te les donnaient en entier,
Et tu feignais de disparaître
Pour qu'elles te crussent dans la mort leur camarade de promotion.
Tu étais de ceux qui élisent l'océan pour domicile comme d'autres
    couchent sous les ponts
Et moi je me cachais les yeux derrière des lunettes noires

TO LAUTRÉAMONT

At random I started digging into the ground hoping you would come
    out
I elbowed away houses and forests to see behind them.
I could spend a whole night waiting for you with the doors and
    windows open,
Two untouched drinks on the table
But you didn't appear,
Lautréamont.

All around me cows were dying of hunger facing cliffs
Turning their obstinate backs to the greenest of fields,
Silently lambs climbed back into the bellies of their mothers bringing
    death.
The dogs deserting America looked back over their shoulders
Because they would have liked to say something before they left.
All alone on the continent,
I looked for you in sleep where meetings are easier
Just stand at a street corner, the other will hasten to get there
But you never appeared,
Lautréamont,
Even behind my closed eyes.
The day I met you across from the Isle of Fernando Noronha,
You had the shape of a wave but more genuine, more circumspect,
Heading for Uruguay without undue haste
The other waves drew back in tribute to your misfortunes,
With only twelve seconds of life spent moving toward death,
They were giving it all to you,
And you pretended to disappear
So they'd think that in death you were graduates of the same class.
People like you choose to live in the ocean the way others sleep under
    bridges
And I was hiding my eyes behind dark glasses

Sur un paquebot où flottait une odeur de femme et de cuisine.
La musique montait aux mâts furieux d'être mêlés aux attouchements
    du tango,
J'avais honte de mon coeur où coulait le sang des vivants,
Alors que tu es mort depuis 1870, et privé du liquide séminal
Tu prends la forme d'une vague pour faire croire que ça t'est égal.

Le jour même de ma mort je te vois venir à moi
Avec ton visage d'homme.
Tu déambules favorablement les pieds nus dans de hautes mottes de ciel,
Mais à peine arrivé à une distance convenable
Tu m'en lances une au visage,
Lautréamont.

1925

On an ocean liner where scents of women mingled with those of
    cooking.
Music rose up to the masts, furious at being involved in disreputable
    tangos,
I was ashamed of my heart which pulsed with the blood of the living,
Because you have been dead since 1870, and deprived of seminal fluid,
You take the form of a wave so we will believe you don't care.

On the very day of my death I see you coming toward me
With your human face.
You stroll encouragingly, barefoot among lofty clumps of the sky,
But when you are just close enough
You hurl one at my face,
Lautréamont.

1925

PT & KM

LA SANGLANTE MÉTAMORPHOSE

Pendant que vous changez cruellement de mains
Je n'ai plus qu'une peau de tristesse sans glose
Et je tâtonne en vain vers la métamorphose
Dans le silence où se forment les assassins.

Affamés l'un de l'autre et mangeant notre faim
Jusqu'à périr, ci-gît à nos pieds le morose.
Coupables! regardez le tribunal sans fin
Òu témoigne à la barre une explicante rose.

Que veut-elle? On entend mal, on est dur d'oreille,
Tant la fleur est obscure en son parler vermeil.
Elle dit ce qu'il faut jusqu'à le ressasser
Dans l'air monumental de plus en plus glacé.

METAMORPHOSIS IN BLOOD

While you put on new hands so cruelly
My last sad skin needs no analysis;
I grope in vain toward metamorphosis
In silence where assassins multiply.

Hungry for each other and eating our fill
To extinction, what's morose has come to die
At our feet. Sinners! Watch the endless trial
Where a rose takes the stand to testify.

To what? And to deaf ears the sounds don't reach
So garbled is this flower's crimson speech,
She makes her point until her story's old,
And the monumental air increasingly cold.

PT & KM

TU DISPARAIS

Tu disparais, déjà te voilà plein de brume
Et l'on rame vers toi comme au travers du soir,
Tu restes seul parmi les ans qui te consument
Dans tes bras la minceur de tes derniers espoirs.

Où tu poses le pied viennent des feuilles mortes
Au souffle faiblissant d'anciennes amours,
La lune qui te suit prend tes dernières forces
Et te bleuit sans fin pour ton ultime jour.

Pourtant l'on voit percer sous ta candeur chagrine
Tout ce peu qui te reste et fait battre ton coeur
Et parfois un sursaut te hausse et t'illumine
Qui suscite en ta nuit des hiboux de splendeurs.

YOU DISAPPEAR

Already closed in mist you disappear
Now as through an evening we must row
Toward your exile among devouring years,
Slender in your arms the last of hope.

There are dead leaves all along your way
Stirred by the failing breath of loves gone by,
The moon behind you steals your strength away
Fading your pallor for the day you die.

Yet what is left to keep your heart alive
Still can penetrate your rueful candor,
And sometimes abrupt, radiant surprise
Awakens from your night the owls of splendor.

PT & KM

JULES SUPERVIELLE

THE OX AND THE DONKEY IN THE MANGER

On the way to Bethlehem the donkey, led by Joseph, was carrying the Virgin: she didn't weigh much, occupied only by the future inside her.

The ox followed, all alone.

In town, the travelers entered an abandoned stable and Joseph instantly got to work.

These men are absolutely amazing, thought the ox. *Look what they accomplish with their hands and arms. Certainly worth more than our hooves and fetlocks. And our master is unequaled at doing odd jobs and organizing things, straightening out what's twisted and twisting what's straight, doing what needs to be done without regret or melancholy.*

Joseph leaves and returns without delay, carrying some straw on his back. But what straw it is, so deep-rooted and sundrenched it's the beginning of a miracle.

What are they preparing over there? the donkey wonders. *You'd think they were making a little bed for a child.*

"You may be needed tonight," says the Virgin to the ox and the donkey.

The animals trade a long look, in an attempt to understand, then they lie down.

A gentle voice, which has just crossed the whole sky, soon awakens them.

The ox gets up, observes that in the crib a naked child is sleeping, and warms him with his breath, methodically, from head to toe.

With a smiling glance, the Virgin thanks him.

Winged creatures enter and leave, pretending not to see the walls they walk through with such ease.

Joseph returns with swaddling clothes, loaned by a neighbor.

"It's marvelous," he says, in his carpenter's voice, a little too loud under the circumstances. "It's midnight and broad daylight. And there are three suns instead of one. But they're trying to merge."

At dawn, the ox gets up, careful where he puts his hooves, afraid he'll wake the child, or crush a heavenly flower, or hurt an angel. How marvelously difficult everything has become!

Neighbors stop by to see Jesus and the Virgin. They are poor people, with nothing to offer but their radiant faces. Then others come, who bring walnuts, a little flute.

The ox and the donkey step back slightly to give them room and wonder what impression they themselves are going to make on the child, who hasn't seen them yet. He has just woken up.

"We aren't monsters," says the donkey.

"But, you know, with our faces, which aren't at all like his or his parents', we could terrify him."

"The crib, the stable, and its beamed roof--they don't have his face either. Yet he wasn't scared of them."

But the ox was not convinced. He thought of his horns and ruminated:

It's really very painful not being able to get near those you love the most without intimidating them. I always have to be careful not to hurt anyone; and yet it isn't in my nature to attack people or things, not without a serious reason. I'm not evil or venomous. But everywhere I go, there go my horns, immediately, and I wake up with them, and even when I'm bleary with sleep and moving in a fog, my bruisers, my two points come along, never neglecting me. And I feel them at the very tip of my dreams, in the middle of the night.

A terrible fear seized the ox at the thought that he'd come so close to the child to warm him up. What if he'd been careless enough to stick him with a horn!

"You mustn't get too near the little one," said the donkey, who had guessed at his companion's thoughts. "Don't even consider it; you'd hurt him. Besides, you might dribble some of that saliva you can hardly control, and that would be a mess. How come you dribble so much, anyway, when you're happy? Keep it to yourself. You don't need to show us all."

(Silence from the ox.)

"But as for me, I'm going to offer him my ears. You understand: they move, they go every which way, there's no bones, they're soft to the touch. They're scary and reassuring at the same time. Just what's needed to amuse a child. And it's instructive at his age."

"Yes I understand, I've never said the contrary. I'm not stupid."

However, since the donkey seemed too pleased with himself, the ox added: "Watch you don't go braying in his face. You'd kill him."

"Peasant!" said the donkey.

The ox is stationed to the right of the crib, the donkey to the left, places they were occupying at the moment of the Nativity and that the ox, liking a certain protocol, particularly favors. Still and deferential, they remain there hours at a time, as if posing for some invisible painter.

The infant lowers his eyelids. He is eager to fall asleep again. A luminous angel is waiting for him several feet beyond sleep, to teach him or perhaps to ask him something.

The living angel steps from Jesus' dream, suddenly present in the stable. After bowing to the newborn, he paints the purest halo around his head. And another for the Virgin, and a third for Joseph. Then he floats off in a dazzlement of wings and feathers whose whiteness, ever-renewed and rustling, resembles that of the tides.

"No halo for us," observes the ox. "Certainly the angel has his reasons. We're too insignificant, the donkey and I. Besides, what have we done to deserve one?"

"You sure didn't do a thing, but you're forgetting that I carried the Virgin."

The ox thinks to himself:

How is it possible that the Virgin, so beautiful and so weightless, was hiding this lovely infant?

But perhaps he's spoken aloud. For the donkey replies:

"There are some things that you can't understand."

"Why are you always saying I don't understand? I've lived longer than you. I've worked in the mountains, on the plains, near the sea."

"That's not the question," says the donkey.

Then:

"It isn't just the halo. I'm sure you didn't notice, ox, that the child is bathed in a kind of marvelous dust. Really, it's better than dust."

"It's much more delicate," says the ox. "It's like light, a golden haze that emanates from his little body."

"Yes, but you're just saying that to make it seem you noticed."

"I didn't?"

The ox pulls the donkey into a corner of the stable where, in token of adoration, the ruminant has arranged a twig delicately encircled by pieces of straw that perfectly depict the radiance of the divine flesh. Here is the first chapel. This straw the ox brought in from outside. He didn't dare touch the straw in the crib: it was so good to eat, he had a superstitious fear of it.

The ox and the donkey went out to graze until nightfall. In the fields, although it usually takes stones so long to understand, many of them already did. The animals even met a pebble who, by a slight change in color and shape, told them he was aleady in the know.

There were also wild flowers who knew and must be spared. It was hard work grazing the countryside without committing sacrilege. Eating without committing sacrilege. And eating seemed increasingly pointless to the ox, sated with happiness.

He also wondered before drinking: *What about this water? Does it know?*

When in doubt, he thought it better not to drink at all and so went farther on, toward muddy water that was obviously still unaware.

At times, nothing alerted him until he felt an infinite sweetness in his throat just as he swallowed.

Too late, thought the ox. *I shouldn't have drunk that.*

He scarcely dared to breathe; the air seemed a sacred thing to him and altogether knowledgeable. He was afraid of breathing in an angel.

It shamed the ox to feel that he was not always as clean as he would have liked: *Well, I'll have to be cleaner than before, that's all. Nothing for it but to pay attention. Watch where I put my feet.*

The donkey felt entirely at ease.

The sun entered the stable, and the two beasts quarreled over the honor of shading the child.

A little sun would probably be harmless, thought the ox, *but the donkey will claim as usual that I just don't get it.*

The child continued to sleep, and sometimes he reflected as he slept, and knit his brows.

One day, with his muzzle, the donkey subtly turned the child a little bit in his direction, while the Virgin was at the door, answering a thousand questions posed by future Christians.

And Mary, approaching her son again, had a terrible fright: she kept on looking for her baby's face where she had left it.

When she understood what had just happened, she told the donkey it wasn't a good idea to touch the child. The ox concurred with a silence of exceptional quality. He knew how to give to his muteness a rhythm, nuances, punctuation. On cold days, you could easily follow the movement of his mind, and see many other things, by the length of the column of breath that streamed from his nostrils.

The ox didn't believe himself authorized to serve the child except indirectly, by attracting any flies in the stable to himself (every morning he went and rubbed his back against a wild beehive) or by crushing insects against the wall.

The donkey listened for noises from outside and when something struck him as suspicious, he barred the entrance. Immediately, the ox got behind him for increased bulk. Both of them made themselves as heavy as possible: while the danger lasted, their heads and stomachs filled up with lead and granite. But their eyes shone more vigilantly than ever.

The ox was amazed to see that when the Virgin drew near the crib, she had the gift of making her baby smile. And despite his beard, Joseph succeeded too without much effort, either by his presence alone or by playing the little flute. The ox would have liked to play something too. All you had to do, really, was breathe.

I don't want to speak ill of the boss, but I don't think that with his breath alone he could have kept the Christ Child warm. And as far as the flute is concerned, all I'd need is to be alone with the little one: in that situation he doesn't intimidate me anymore. He turns back into a creature who needs protecting. And an ox does feel his own strength, after all.

When they went into the fields together, it often happened that the ox left the donkey.

"Now where are you going?"

"Be right back."

"Where are you going?" insisted the donkey.

"I'm going to see that he doesn't need anything. You never know."

"Why can't you leave him in peace!"

The ox disappeared. In the stable there was a kind of skylight—what people later called a bull's eye, for this very reason—through which the bovine could look in from the outside.

One day, the ox observed that Mary and Joseph were gone. He found the little flute on a bench, within reach of his muzzle, neither too close nor too far from the Child.

What can I play him? wondered the ox, who didn't dare approach Jesus' ear except by means of this musical intermediary. *A work song? The warrior song of a courageous little bull? Or the enchanted heifer?*

Often oxen pretend to be chewing their cud, when really, in the depths of their soul, they are singing.

The ox blew delicately into the flute, and it's by no means clear he needed help from an angel to achieve such purity of sound. In his crib the child raised his head and shoulders slightly to see. The flutist, however, wasn't pleased with the result, although at least he felt sure he had not been heard outside. He was mistaken.

Quickly he fled, for fear that someone, especially the donkey, might come in and catch him too close to the little flute.

"Come see him," said the Virgin to the ox, one day. "Why don't you get near my child anymore, you who warmed him so well when he was still stark naked?"

Emboldened, the ox stood close to Jesus, who took hold of his muzzle with both hands, to put him at his ease. The ox restrained his breath, un-needed now. Jesus smiled. The ox's joy was silent. It had taken the very form of his body and now it filled him to the tips of his horns.

The child looked at the donkey and the ox, one by one: the donkey a little too self-confident; and the ox who felt himself of an extraordinary opacity beside this face illuminated delicately from within, as if a lamp were seen through finespun curtains, passing from one room to another, in a tiny distant dwelling.

Seeing the ox so gloomy, the child burst out laughing.

The beast didn't fully understand this laughter and wondered if the child weren't making fun of him. Must he appear more reserved from now on? Or even go away?

Then the child laughed again, and his laughter was so luminous, so fil-ial, it seemed to the ox, that he saw he'd been right to stay.

Often the Virgin and her son looked at each other, up close. And they vied for who was proudest of the other.

It seems to me that all this should be pure joy, mused the ox. *Never has there been a purer mother, a more beautiful child. Yet how solemn they seem at times, both of them!*

The ox and the donkey were getting ready to return to the stable. After having really looked, for fear of being mistaken, the ox said: "Check out the star crossing the sky. It's so beautiful it warms my heart."

"Leave your heart out of this, it has nothing to do with the great events that we've been seeing lately."

"You can say what you like, I do believe that star is coming toward us. Look how low it is in the sky. As though it were aiming at our stable. And beneath it are three characters covered with precious gems."

The beasts were almost on the threshold of the stable:

"What do you think is going to happen, ox?"

"You ask too much, donkey. I'm happy with what *is*. That's already a lot."

"Personally, I have an idea."

"Come on, come on!" Joseph said to them, opening the door. "Don't you see you're obstructing the entrance and keeping these individuals from proceeding?"

The beasts moved aside to let the Magi pass. They were three in number and one of them, black from head to toe, represented Africa. At first, the ox kept a discreet eye on him, wanting to make sure his intentions were entirely honorable toward the newborn.

When the black man (who must have been somewhat nearsighted) bent over to see Jesus close up, his face, polished and shiny as a mirror, reflected the image of the Child, and with such deference, so great a self-forgetting, that the ox's heart was shot through with sweetness.

He's a very good man, thought the ox. *The other two couldn't have done that.*

He added, a few moments later: *And he's the best of the three.*

The ox had just caught the white kings as they carefully slipped into their bags a piece of straw they'd lifted from the crib. The black wise man had taken nothing.

Side by side, on an improvised bed lent by the neighbors, the kings went to sleep.

Strange to keep your crown on while you sleep, thought the ox. *That hard thing must get in the way much more than horns. And with all those brilliant jewels on your head, it must be difficult to doze off.*

They slept nice and quietly, like statues laid out on tombs. And their star shone above the manger.

Immediately before daybreak all three got up at once, their movements identical. They had just beheld the same angel in a dream, who recommended that they leave immediately and that they not return to Herod the jealous to tell him they had seen the Christ Child.

They departed, leaving the star to shine above the manger so that all knew clearly where it was.

The Ox's Prayer

You mustn't judge me, heavenly Infant, by my stunned, unfeeling look. If only I could someday stop resembling a little rock that's plodding forward!

These horns, as you must surely know, are more ornament than anything else. I'll even admit to you I've never used them.

Jesus, shed a little of your light on the confusion and the poverty inside me. Teach me a little of your delicacy, you whose tiny feet and hands are so meticulously fastened to your body. Will you tell me, little Sir, why one day all I had to do was turn my head to see you whole? I thank you so, that I am able to be on my knees before you, marvelous Child, and to live like this, familiarly, with angels and with stars! I wonder sometimes if you were misinformed, if it's really me who should be here; perhaps you haven't noticed that I have a big scar on my back and that a patch of hair is missing on one side. It isn't pretty. Without even seeking further than my family, my brother could have been selected to be here, or my cousins, who are much better-looking than I am. Wouldn't the lion or the eagle have been more appropriate?

"Hold your tongue," said the donkey. "What have you got to sigh about like that, can't you see you're keeping him awake with all your ruminating?"

He's right, the ox said to himself. *You've got to know when it's time to shut up, even if you feel a happiness so huge you don't know where to put it.*

But the donkey was praying too:

"Donkeys that pull between the shafts, donkeys that pack burdens, life is going to be beautiful beneath our steps, and foals will await the course of events in festive pastures. Thanks to you, little youth, stones will remain in their rightful places by the side of the road, they won't come falling down on us. Another thing. Why should there still be mountains, or even hills, along our route? Wouldn't plains do, everywhere, for everyone? And how come the ox who is stronger than I am never carries anybody on his back? And how come my ears are so long and I have no hair on my tail and my hooves are so little and my chest is narrow and my voice the color of bad weather? But maybe things don't have to be that way?"

During the nights that followed, sometimes one star and sometimes another stood guard. And sometimes whole constellations. To keep the sky's secret, a cloud always took up the space where the absent stars should have been. And it was a marvel to see how the Infinitely Distant Ones got altogether tiny, in order to take their places above the manger, and kept within themselves their excessive heat and light and their immensity, giving off only what was necessary to warm and illuminate the stable, without frightening the child. First nights of Christianity… Back then, the Virgin, Joseph, the Child, the Ox and the Donkey were extraordinarily themselves. Their own likeness, which dispersed a little during the day and dissipated around visitors, assumed a miraculous concentration and safety after sunset.

Through the ox and the donkey, several animals asked to meet the Christ Child. And one day a horse known for his sociability and speed was appointed by the ox, with Joseph's consent, to convene all those who wanted to come on the following day.

The donkey and the ox wondered if ferocious beasts would be allowed in, and what about dromedaries, camels, elephants, all those creatures whose humps, trunks and surplus bones and flesh made them a little suspect?

The same question arose about dreadful insects like scorpions, tarantulas, great wolf spiders, vipers, all those whose glands produce venom night and day and even in the purity of dawn.

The Virgin did not hesitate.

"Let them all in. My child is as safe in his crib as he would be on high."

"But one by one!" Joseph added, in an almost military tone. "I don't want two creatures coming in the door at once, it will be utter chaos."

They began with the venomous beasts, since it was felt that they were owed this reparation. Much was made of the tact with which the snakes avoided looking at the Virgin, giving her person as wide a berth as possible. And they exited with as much calm and dignity as if they'd been doves or guard dogs.

There were also creatures so small that it was hard to know if they were there or still waiting outside. A whole hour was allowed the atoms to introduce themselves and circle around the crib. When their time was up, although from the slight prickling of his skin Joseph sensed they weren't all gone yet, he ordered the next animals to appear.

The dogs couldn't keep themselves from indicating their surprise: they hadn't been allowed into the stable permanently like the ox and the donkey. Everybody petted them, in response. And so they withdrew, filled with visible gratitude.

However, when the lion's approach was announced by his smell, the ox and the donkey grew uneasy. All the more so, since this odor cavalierly cut through the incense and myrrh and other perfumes sprinkled everywhere by the Wise Men.

The ox appreciated the generosity that underlay Joseph and the Virgin's trust. But to place a child, this fragile radiance, so close to a beast whose breath could easily extinguish him with a single puff...

The anxiety felt by the ox and donkey was all the greater since they understood that decency required they remain entirely immobile in the lion's presence. They could no more think of attacking him than they could the thunder or the lightning. And the ox, weakened by fasting, felt more ethereal than combative.

The lion entered with his mane, which none but the desert wind had combed, and with melancholy eyes that said: *I am the lion, what can I do about it? I am only the king of beasts.*

You could see his chief concern was to take up the least possible amount of room in the stable and that it wasn't easy for him to breathe in and out without disturbing everything around him, nor to forget his long retractile claws, his jawbone powered by its potent muscles. He advanced with lowered eyes, hiding his admirable teeth as if they were a shameful malady, and with such modesty that it was obvious he belonged to that race of lions who would one day refuse to devour Saint Blandine. The Virgin took pity and tried to reassure him with the same smile she reserved for her child. The lion looked straight ahead of him and seemed to say, in an even more despairing tone than ever:

What have I done to be this big and strong? You well know I've never eaten except when pushed to it by hunger and fresh air. And you will understand, too, there was the question of the cubs. Almost all of us have tried to be herbivorous. But grass just isn't made for us. It clogs us up.

Then his enormous head, like an explosion of hair and fur, bowed down and sadly touched the hard earth, and the brush at the end of his tail seemed as despondent as his head, in the midst of so great a silence that it hurt everyone.

When it was the tiger's turn, he flattened himself out on the ground until, by dint of mortifications and austerities, he had become a veritable bedside rug at the foot of the crib. Then, in an instant, he snapped himself together with incredible precision and elasticity, and left without further ado.

The giraffe exhibited its hooves in the doorway for a long moment, and everyone was unanimous in considering that "that counted" as walking around the crib.

Same for the elephant: he contented himself with kneeling before the threshold and sweeping his trunk back and forth like a sort of censer bearer, which everybody very much enjoyed.

An immensely woolly sheep insisted he be sheared, then and there: they left him his fleece, while thanking him.

The mother kangaroo wished at all costs to give Jesus one of her offspring, claiming she was offering this gift with all her heart, it was no deprivation, she had other little kangaroos at home. But Joseph didn't see it that way, and she had to carry back her child.

The ostrich was more fortunate: she profited from a moment of inattention to lay an egg in the corner and leave without a word. A souvenir they found only the next morning. The donkey discovered it. He had never seen anything so fat or hard, by way of eggs, and thought it was a miracle. But Joseph did his best to disabuse him: he made an omelette of it.

The fish, being unable to appear, given their deplorable respiratory problems out of the water, had delegated a seagull to replace them.

SELECTED PROSE AND POETRY

The birds left behind them their songs, the pigeons their love affairs, the monkeys their pranks, the cats their gaze, the turtle doves the sweetness of their throats.

And others, too, would have liked to introduce themselves--animals not yet discovered who are waiting for a name down in the bosom of the earth or sea, at such depths that for them it's always night, without stars, moon or change of season.

You could sense beating in the air the souls of those who could not come or who were late, and others who lived at the ends of the earth but nonetheless set out on tiny insect feet, insects so small they couldn't have progressed more than a meter in one hour, but whose lives were so short they could only hope for fifty centimeters—and even then, only with extraordinary luck.

There were miracles: the tortoise hurried, the iguana slowed down, the hippopotamus was graceful in its genuflections, the parrots kept quiet.

A little before sunset, one incident upset everybody. Tired from having directed the procession all day long and not having taken any food at all, Joseph crushed a nasty spider with his foot, forgetting that she'd come to pay homage to the Child. And the saint's deeply distressed face dismayed everyone for quite some time.

Certain creatures from whom one might have expected more discretion overstayed their welcome in the stable: the ox had to dismiss the weasel, the squirrel, and the badger, who didn't want to leave.

Several crepuscular butterflies remained, profiting from their color, which resembled that of the roof beams, to spend the whole night above the crib. But the next day the first ray of sun betrayed them, and as Joseph didn't want to favor anybody he immediately chased them off.

Some flies, also invited to withdraw, let it be known by their unwillingness to go that they had always been there, and Joseph couldn't think what to tell them.

The supernatural apparitions among whom the ox was living often took his breath away. And having developed the habit of holding it, in the manner of Asian ascetics, he too became a visionary, and although less at ease with grandeur than humility, he experienced real ecstasies. But he was too scrupulous to invent saints and angels. He only saw them if they were really in his vicinity.

Poor me, thought the bovine, alarmed by these apparitions, which he considered suspect, *poor me, I'm just a beast of burden, maybe even the devil. Why do I have horns like his, I who have never done evil? What if I'm only a sorcerer?*

Joseph couldn't help noticing the anxiety of the ox, who was getting visibly thinner.

"Go outside and eat something!" he cried. "Here you are, underfoot all day long. Soon you'll be nothing more than skin and bones."

The donkey and the ox went out.

"It's true you're skinny," said the donkey. "Your bones have got so pointy that horns are going to sprout all over your body."

"Don't mention horns to me!"

And the ox said to himself:

Yes, he's right, one has to live. Here, eat this lovely tuft of green. And this one? Do you imagine it's poisonous? No, I'm just not hungry. How very beautiful the Child is! And those huge figures coming in and out and breathing with their ever-beating wings. All that heavenly high society that enters our simple stable, without even getting dirty. Come on, ox, don't think about that—eat something. And listen, you mustn't let yourself be woken up by happiness when it comes tweaking your ears in the middle of the night. Nor spend so much time near the crib on just one knee, in order to make it hurt. You've rubbed your hide off at the joint; one minute more and the flies are going to land on it.

There came a night when the constellation Taurus was to be on duty above the manger, across a section of black sky. Aldebaran's red eye glimmered, magnificent and ablaze, nearby. And the horns and flanks of Taurus were decorated with enormous gems. The ox was proud to see the Child so well-guarded. Everyone slept peacefully, the donkey with lowered, trusting ears. But the ox, although strengthened by the supernatural presence of the constellation, his relative and friend, was filled with weakness. He thought of his sacrifices for the Child, his useless vigils, his ridiculous protectiveness.

Did the constellation Taurus see me? he wondered. *That big red starry eye, which shines so hard it's scary, does he know I'm here? Those stars, so high, so distant you can't even tell which way they're looking.*

Suddenly Joseph, who's been tossing and turning in his bed for several minutes, stands up, his arms raised to the heavens. He who usually seems moderate in gesture and word, here he is waking everybody up, even the Child.

"I saw the Lord in a dream. We must leave here without delay. Because of Herod, yes, who wants to attack Jesus."

The Virgin picks up her son as if the King of the Jews were already in the doorway, right there, a butcher knife in his hand.

The donkey gets to his feet.

"And that one?" Joseph says to the Virgin, indicating the ox.

"It seems to me he's just too weak to come with us."

The ox tries to show them it's not true. He makes an enormous effort to stand up, but never has he felt more tethered to the ground. So, begging for help, he looks at the constellation Taurus. He can only count on it now for the strength to leave. But the celestial bovine doesn't move a muscle, his eye still just as red and flaming, his profile still turned toward the ox.

"He hasn't eaten in several days," the Virgin says to Joseph.

Oh, I understand completely why they're going to leave me here! thinks the ox. *It was too good to be true, it couldn't last. Besides, on the road I'd be no more than a bony obsolete ghost. All my ribs are sick of my skin and ask only to take it easy under the sky.*

The donkey approaches the ox and rubs his muzzle against the ruminant's, to let him know the Virgin just entrusted him to a neighbor and he will lack for nothing after their departure. But the ox, his eyes half-closed, seems absolutely crushed.

The Virgin strokes him and cries, "Listen, we're not going away, of course not. It was simply to scare you!"

"That goes without saying. We'll be right back," adds Joseph. "People don't set off for faraway in the middle of the night."

"The night's so beautiful," the Virgin continues, "we're going to take advantage of it to give the child some air. He's a little pale these days."

"Perfectly true," says the holy man.

This is a white lie. The ox understands and does not wish to hamper the travelers' preparations, so he pretends to fall into a deep sleep. It's his way of lying.

"He's fallen asleep," says the Virgin. "Let's put the straw from the manger right next to him, so he won't have need of anything when he wakes up. And leave the little flute within reach of his breath," she goes on, very quietly. "He really likes to play it when he's alone."

They start to go. The stable door creaks.

I should have oiled it, thinks Joseph, afraid of waking the ox. But the latter is still feigning sleep.

They close the door carefully.

While the donkey in the manger gradually becomes the donkey of the flight into Egypt, the ox stays behind, his eyes staring at the straw where recently the Christ Child lay.

He knows that he will never touch the little flute again.

The constellation Taurus rejoins the zenith at a bound and with one tap of its horn fastens itself to the sky, in the place it will never leave again.

When the neighbor enters, a little after dawn, the ox has stopped ruminating.

NK

THE FLIGHT INTO EGYPT

The Child had awoken at the moment of departure when the Virgin, who was on the donkey, took him from Joseph's arms.

"Is he asleep?" asked the carpenter, a little later.

"Oh yes!"

"Poor little baby, this was the best thing to do."

They went forward, illuminated not too much, not too little, by the moon in its first crescent. Stars watched, unwavering, as they passed by, and an astronomer with all his gear would not have noticed anything unusual in the celestial vault.

Joseph had worried that the child's head might be encircled by a halo on their trip, as in the manger. Happily, nothing of the kind was shining. God had approved of darkness for their move. And the angels were displaying extraordinary restraint. There was not the slightest question of an escort on their part, and if from time to time the clouds assumed angelic shapes, it was done with such discretion that you couldn't reasonably reproach heaven.

Dawn lightly brushes the horizon. No one on the road. Nothing but a poor desiccated palm tree.

So much the better, thinks Joseph. *I don't trust talkers, even well-intentioned.*

As they are passing the palm, it bends its only knee and bows down in the dust.

This gesture makes the Child laugh; he's just been awakened by the first ray of sunshine. And the Virgin thinks it makes a very pretty picture.

"Don't you see this couldn't be more dangerous?" cries Joseph, in a voice he tries to muffle, unsuccessfully. "If trees start paying homage, I give Herod less than two hours to find us."

"God is protecting us," says the Virgin. "The absence of halos proves it."

"Of course he's protecting us. Still, all that's needed is a bunch of brainless trees calling us to everyone's attention."

And there on the horizon stood a whole little forest, right next to a thriving town, which really worried the head of the family. Would those trees know enough to stay in place or would they suddenly step forward in potentially lethal admiration?

When he was level with the grove of palms, the child began to stare at them mischievously, as though to egg them on to imitate their religious comrade.

"Hide the Child in your cape," groused Joseph.

Mary paid no attention; she had faith. And not one tree moved. Only three doves, of a suspiciously excessive whitenesss, kept the Holy Family company for part of the way.

Never a moment's peace, thought Joseph. *If there'd been one wagging tongue in the neighborhood, the Child was done for.*

And all the while the Innocents were being massacred, in the hope that Jesus was among them.

Two or three at a time, Herod's emissaries entered the houses, bringing with them terrible cruel children whose job it was to ferret out those of their own age. At the end of a seemingly casual visit, they killed your son for you on the spot, as though he were a viper. And they departed, seeking with their eyes some unimaginably sinister *thank you.* Even one of Herod's own sons, taken in to nurse in Bethlehem, was murdered, in pursuance of his father's orders.

Once identified, the executioners soon reappeared disguised as beggars or shepherds, businessmen or charitable ladies.

People carefully hid everything that might betray a child's presence in the house: toys, little articles of clothing, shoes. To leave around the tiniest of these objects was as good as saying, *Do please kill my child for me right now.* And neighbors were not wrong to comment, "Aren't you ashamed, you murderers!" to those negligent parents who left a wooden horse beside their door, or a little trumpet. In order to fool the authorities, mothers often dressed their children in men's clothing. You even saw faint-hearted sixteen-year-olds gluing on false whiskers, and girls who had quite ample bosoms padding them, although nobody with a grain of sense could possibly have taken them for children.

Day and night the massacre continued. And it was pitiful to see this brand new human blood spilled with such unheard-of violence, the little bodies suddenly drained of plans and memories, victims of horrible wounds ten times too big for a child.

Joseph and the Virgin knew all this: people talked of nothing else on the roads of Judea, where every being below a certain age attracted as much attention as a highwayman.

And Joseph hastened to get to Egypt, taking unfrequented roads.

Meanwhile, almost immediately after the Child's departure, the soul of the ox in the Manger escaped through the stable's bull's eye window, avoiding the wide door by which the Family had left.

Outside, its first thought was: *I don't have a head or hooves, I am the soul of the ox I used to be.* And a little after that: *I'm like a breeze in the sky. No need to graze or sleep.* To tell the truth, it didn't yet know what to do with all this marvelous lightness.

Encountering no air resistance, souls are able to move much faster than bodies, and the ox's soul soon saw the Virgin, Joseph, the Child and the donkey on the road, all still saddened by the condition of the creature they'd had to abandon in the stable.

There they are, thought the ox, joyfully. *It's them all right, with each part of their body in its customary place. Oh, how nice they look on the road, so much like themselves, undiminished, understated! Just to have seen this! All my efforts are repaid.*

And he went from one to another, counting them and speaking to them familiarly, in his altogether silent fashion. But no matter how you try not to be pushy, there always comes a moment when you'd really like people to know that you exist, that you can see and hear.

Circling the donkey, he thought: *We two know each other so well, it's impossible he won't recognize me.* But the donkey doesn't notice anything bovine around him. So the ox, like the lightest of birds, lands on the baby's shoulder. He is nothing more than air and finds himself without a thing to say.

"I still can't get over it," says the Virgin to Joseph. "Leaving behind that poor weak animal in the stable." *Maybe this,* thinks the ox, *is the start of a conversation that will end with my being discovered.* But the Virgin continues: "Certainly by this time the unfortunate creature is as dead as can be. Unless… He was so filled with charity, perhaps he too has a soul."

"Stop talking nonsense, you silly woman."

And so rapid is repentance among Saints that he immediately adds: "Forgive me for 'nonsense.'"

"And for 'silly woman,'" says the Virgin.

The Christ Child turned around from time to time as if he were searching the road for the ox, when what was left of the latter hovered in front of him. And the ox said to himself: *Will I never get them to understand I'm here? Well, maybe it's better that way. The dead are one thing. The living, another. The dead must know their place and how to stay there, dignified, not always trying to escape it. Let's help them to forget me. Maybe self-effacement is the truest sign of courtesy and charity. But how uncertain you feel that you can actually stay in one place when you are only a soul! Always at the mercy of a sudden breeze, a thunderclap, here in this country where storms are so frequent. I don't doubt I'm indestructible these days, but so light that the travelers' least breath makes me fly off at random; when the donkey sniffed a while ago, he nearly breathed me in.*

And how could the ox, who'd always been a fan of balance, even of a certain heaviness, like all those of his race—how could he not have been afflicted by this distressing to-and-fro?

Meanwhile the Virgin, upset at their abrupt departure from Bethlehem, was not able to feed the Child as she wished. Jesus didn't fuss, of course, but he was secretly sucking his thumb, you could tell. And asking for milk at a farm presented the greatest of dangers: people were immediately inclined to search your luggage for a child.

The ox flew from one traveler to the next like la Fontaine's horsefly outside the coach. Alive, he had so suffered from being unable to do anything serious for the baby and it was happening again in death.

As he was roaming the countryside, never losing the travelers from view, he spotted a young cow, faraway, whose strange friskiness caught his attention. He approached her, thinking that perhaps someone of his own race would understand him better, and surprised himself by murmuring in the stranger's ear: "Young cow, won't you please help me find some shelter? Make a tiny place for me beneath your skin. I won't hurt you." And he was stunned to hear the cow say in response: "Who are you, anyway?"

"I am the wandering soul of an ox."

"And why'd you pick me in particular to make a place for you beneath my skin? Be aware, ox, that I take up all the room myself. My skin is an entirely personal envelope. I wouldn't loan it to my best friend."

"You won't even know I'm there! Besides which, you might need someone. You can sometimes be very much alone in your own skin."

"No, no, that's all talk from a wandering soul. Move right along, ox. I don't even know you."

SELECTED PROSE AND POETRY

But the cow was starting to give in. The ox thought that it might be worth a try somewhere around her nostrils. And benefiting from a moment when she drew in air, he unceremoniously entered the ruminant's head.

"Hey! I know you're in there now," the cow said. "But I'm warning you, if you cause me the slightest inconvenience, you're out of there."

This may not be so easy, thought the bovine soul, in an aside. (But was an aside even possible now?) *I'm nothing more than a spirit inhabiting flesh that isn't mine. We'll wait and see.*

Instantly the ox took steps to influence this uncouth, slightly crazy body of a cow, civilizing it, catechizing it for the greater good of all. Since he never left the heart and mind of his hostess, he quickly persuaded her that she must gallop through the countryside to rejoin the ox's old masters.

"Don't turn around," says Joseph to the Virgin. "We're being followed."

From a sense of duty, he himself turns. And right away the cow stops near the Child, and points a horn at her udders, swollen with milk.

The Virgin says, "You can milk this fine little cow."

"But she's giving us away with her odd attentions."

"Here, use this bowl, my baby's hungry" is the Virgin's only response.

Suspicious, hidden inside a cloak, Joseph won't stop milking the cow and tasting the milk, as though it were a matter of some bizarre medicine. Then the Virgin takes the bowl out of his hands, swallows two mouthfuls, declares there's nothing diabolical about the liquid and gives some to the Child, who looks elsewhere to show he's in no hurry.

But as for Joseph, visibly nervous, he is picturing the journey of this suspect milk into the mouth and little person of the Child.

"To you, it all seems natural," he tells the Virgin, moodily. "If a hundred cows offered us their udders, you'd find that just fine too."

"There aren't a hundred, only one."

"Obviously, Mary. I can count. But I wonder if we're right accepting this beast's services, even if she really does mean well. Just think for a minute of how many animals paid homage to the Child after his birth. What if the ostrich and the giraffe and the lion and all the others started following us down the road? What a giveaway to Herod's police!"

The Child was now considering the cow with unusual sympathy.

"Don't look over there!" said Joseph, as if the devil himself were present, with four hooves and the muzzle of a cow.

"The poor innocent, why don't you want him to look at her?"

And Jesus began to laugh with joy, seeing the cow approach so he could touch her muzzle, just as he used to do with the ox in the Manger. For him, in fact, the ox and cow were one and the same beast. Marvelous, the power of confusion in a child, which permitted him to see so clearly.

"One day," said Joseph, his mind finally at rest, "we'll explain to him the difference between a true martyr like the ox and an animal who may be well-intentioned but without true greatness."

Nonetheless the Virgin too had started petting the good little dairy-maid, who was part of their journey from then on. Despite the exhortations of the bovine spirit, sometimes she fidgeted while being milked. And one day, her impatience irritated Joseph so much that, hiding from everybody else for fear of giving a bad example, he kicked the empty air, as Saints do when they aren't pleased (and don't want to commit a sin).

And the ox's soul thought: *Excellent Joseph, how you'd suffer knowing that I saw you kick.*

The donkey had never liked cows—he thought them overwrought, muddleheaded, and much too pleased with their teats—but caught himself living with pleasure in the company of this one. It was not so much friendship as a happy acceptance of imposed proximity. Since his separation from the ox, he no longer felt any need to communicate with other animals. He was like a man who has decided he will smoke his pipe in silence all the rest of his days, drawing from it little puffs so imperceptible they seem to issue from the soul, not the body.

The journey continued without harm to the Child. Joseph had come to see the presence of this tag-along cow as a miracle of real worth and even recognized she'd done more for all three of them than the ox, although of course in Joseph's eyes this did nothing to diminish the rare value of the creature they'd abandoned in the stable.

Never had the ox been as comfortable in his own skin as in the cow's; his present usefulness had even cured him of his nearly pathological modesty. Although he didn't regret any of his past sacrifices, he now thought that he might have made them count more. He went so far as to believe that instead of letting himself die of grief, he should have traveled incognito to Jerusalem, while he'd still had the strength, and gored Herod during one of his morning constitutionals. But just how much of this idea was the ox's? Hadn't it been suggested to him by his sister under the skin?

Meanwhile the Romans were requisitioning any livestock on the roads, and they asked Joseph where he'd got his cow. Not wishing to lie, he blushed and said, "She just began to follow us and offered us her udders." They threatened them all with jail if he didn't give a more reasonable answer. Happily, the Virgin with her deeply innocent gaze disarmed the soldiers who encircled them.

"These people are simpletons," the Roman officer concluded. "Let's just take the cow and let them go their way."

They hit the beast and forced her to turn North by means of a rope around her neck and random kicks. In order to remain beside the child, the ox's soul tried vainly to escape her friendly body. But really he and she were one, and he felt caught in her flesh like a fly in glue. He could only get the cow to turn her head a few times toward the baby, all the while doing his best to share the sufferings of the mistreated beast.

Joseph and the Virgin walked for one or two more days in their anxiety, and then quite naturally the halos reappeared around their heads—and the Child's—to show them they had nothing left to fear. Besides which, people had stopped talking on the road about the massacre of the Innocents, and the travelers they met looked more and more Egyptian.

NK

47 BOULEVARD LANNES

À Marcel Jouhandeau

Boulevard Lannes que fais-tu si haut dans l'espace
Et tes tombereaux que tirent des percherons l'un derrière l'autre,
Les naseaux dans l'éternité
Et la queue balayant l'aurore?
Le charretier suit, le fouet levé,
Une bouteille dans sa poche.
Chaque chose a l'air terrestre et vit dans son naturel.
Boulevard Lannes que fais-tu au milieu du ciel
Avec tes immeubles de pierre que viennent flairer les années,
Si à l'écart du soleil de Paris et de sa lune
Que le réverbère ne sait plus s'il faut qu'il s'éteigne ou s'allume
Et que la laitière se demande si ce sont bien des maisons,
Avançant de vrais balcons,
Et si tintent à ses doigts des flacons de lait ou des mondes?
Près du ruisseau un balayeur de feuilles mortes de platanes
En forme un tas pour la fosse commune de tous les platanes
Échelonnés dans le ciel.
Ses mouvements font un bruit aéré d'immensité
Que l'âme voudrait imiter.
Ce chien qui traverse la chaussée miraculeusement
Est-ce encor un chien respirant?
Son poil sent la foudre et la nue
Mais ses yeux restent ingénus
Dans la dérivante atmosphère
Et je doute si le boulevard
N'est pas plus large que l'espace entre le Cygne et Bételgeuse.
Ah! si je colle l'oreille à l'immobile chaussée
C'est l'horrible galop des mondes, la bataille des vertiges;
Par la fente des pavés
Je vois que s'accroche une étoile
À sa propre violence
Dans l'air creux insaisissable
Qui s'enfuit de toutes parts.

47 BOULEVARD LANNES

To Marcel Jouhandeau

Boulevard Lannes, what are you doing so high up in space
Your wagons too, pulled by Percherons, one behind the other,
Their nostrils in eternity
Their tails sweeping the dawn?
The driver follows, his whip held high,
A bottle in his pocket.
Everything looks down-to-earth and lives according to its nature.
Boulevard Lannes, what are you doing in the middle of the sky,
With your stone buildings the years take the scent of as they go by,
So far away from the Paris sun and from its moon
The street lamp wonders whether it's time to turn itself off or on
And the woman delivering milk isn't sure those are really houses
Holding out real balconies,
And is that clinking at her fingertips coming from bottles or worlds?
Close to the gutter a man sweeping the dead leaves of plane trees
Piles them up into a common grave for all the plane trees
Lined up across the sky.
His movements make a noise rustling with immensity
The way the soul would like to sound.
That dog so miraculously crossing the street
Is he still living and breathing?
His coat smells of lightning and high cloud,
But his eyes are still ingenuous
In the shifting atmosphere
And I don't doubt that the boulevard
Is wider than the space between The Swan and Betelgeuse.
Ah! If I put my ear to the motionless street,
The horrible galloping of worlds, the warfare of vertigos;
In the gap between paving stones
I see a star clinging
To its own violence
Through the hollow intangible air
Which flees in all directions.

JULES SUPERVIELLE

113

Caché derrière un peu de nuit comme par une colonne,
En étouffant ma mémoire qui pourrait faire du bruit,
Je guette avec mes yeux d'homme
Mes yeux venus jusqu'ici,
Par quel visage travestis?
Autour de moi je vois bien que c'est l'année où nous sommes
Et cependant on dirait le premier jour du monde
Tant les choses se regardent fixement
Entourées d'un mutisme différent.

Ce pas lourd sur le trottoir
Je le reconnais c'est le mien,
Je l'entends partir au loin,
Il s'est séparé de moi
(Ne lui suis-je donc plus rien)
S'en va maintenant tout seul,
Et se perd au fond du Bois.
Si je crie on n'entend rien
Que la plainte de la Terre
Palpant vaguement sa sphère
À des millions de lieues.
S'assurant de ses montagnes,
De ses fleuves, ses forêts
Attisant sa flamme obscure
Où se chauffe le futur
(Il attend que son tour vienne).

Je reste seul avec mes os
Dont j'entends les blancheurs confuses:
"Où va-t-il entre deux ciels, si froissé par ses pensées,
Si loin de la terre ferme
Le voilà qui cherche l'ombre et qui trouve du soleil."

Puisque je reconnais la face de ma demeure dans cette altitude
Je vais accrocher les portraits de mon père et de ma mère
Entre deux étoiles tremblantes,
Je poserai la pendule ancienne du salon

Hidden behind just enough night to make a column,
Stifling my memory, to keep it quiet,
My human eyes are on watch,
My eyes that have come this far,
Disguised by what face?
Looking around I can see that this is the year we're in,
And yet it seems to be the first day of the world
So steadily do all things look at each other
From within whatever keeps silence differently.

Those heavy footsteps on the sidewalk
I recognize them, they're mine,
I hear them go far away,
Separating from me
(Don't I matter anymore?)
Going off all by themselves,
They get lost deep in the Bois.
If I shriek, nothing is heard
Except the lament of the Earth
Getting vaguely in touch with its orbit
Millions of miles away,
Checking on its mountains,
Its rivers, its forests
Turning up its dark flame
Where the future keeps warm
(Awaiting its turn).

I stay alone with my bones
And their audible wondering whiteness:
"Where is he going between two skies, so annoyed by his thoughts,
So far from solid ground
Now he is looking for shade and he finds the sun."

Since this altitude has shown me the face of my home,
I'll hang the portraits of my father and my mother
Between two trembling stars,
I'll put the antique living room clock

Sur une cheminée taillée dans la nuit dure
Et le savant qui un jour les découvrira dans le ciel
En chuchotera jusqu'à sa mort.
Mais il faudra très longtemps pour que ma main aille et vienne
Comme si elle manquait d'air, de lumière et d'amis
Dans le ciel endolori
Qui faiblement se plaindra
Sous les angles des objets qui seront montés de la Terre.

On a mantelpiece carved from hard night,
And the astronomer who some day finds them in the sky
Will talk of it in a whisper until he dies.
But it will take a very long time for my hand to come and go
As if it found not enough air, light and friends
In the aching sky
Which will quietly complain
Beneath the angular objects rising up from the Earth.

PT & KM

DANS LA FORÊT SANS HEURES

Dans la forêt sans heures
On abat un grand arbre.
Un vide vertical
Tremble en forme de fût
Près du tronc étendu.

Cherchez, cherchez, oiseaux,
La place de vos nids
Dans ce haut souvenir
Tant qu'il murmure encore.

NO HOURS IN THE FOREST

No hours in the forest
A tall tree cut down
A vertical space
Trembles column-like
Near the trunk on the ground.

Hurry, birds, hurry,
Find your nests
In this lofty memory
While it's murmuring still.

PT & KM

THE LITTLE WOOD

You could stroll through this wood for years in safety. And then, one fine day when your time was up, you too turned into a tree. Even if you died in your bed, one more trunk would appear in the little wood. And everyone knew it was you. Really, no one hesitated. In front of this or that tree, everyone agreed it was Aunt Felicia or Uncle John. You could tell from faraway, thanks to a certain indefinable resemblance between tree and human. A child would not have been mistaken. And yet this resemblance wasn't obvious. It was much subtler; it was essential. Aunt Felicia, for example, was a great big sergeant major of a woman and in dying she had given birth to this shriveled little growth:

"That's really her?"

"Gotta believe it, since we all agree."

If someone from the region was dying faraway, at that very instant a new tree would appear in the little wood. As when a missionary died in a distant land. At first, people wondered just who this tree might represent. It didn't resemble anyone. The monk, who had no family, had long ago left and no one remembered him. Then, from China, the news reached home announcing the divine's death on the birthday of the new tree.

Yes, in appearance the wood was just like any other. Nothing to suggest the sadness of cemeteries; it budded in the spring and shed its leaves in autumn, like all the little woods in France…

One day, two young people announced their imminent suicide and disappeared, the boy's father having refused his consent to their marriage. But there was no new tree in the little wood, even though a registered letter arrived at the local police station, signed by the two parties concerned, who planned to kill themselves.

A week went by; no tree. And everybody in the region disapproved so strongly that a little riot took place outside the father's house: he was well-known for his intransigence.

How was it possible, when even the least interesting of people had *their* tree, that "these poor dears were deprived of their own corner in the little wood"? It was scarcely credible. Why had this father been unyielding to such a degree that he had paralyzed the young people like this, even on the other side of life, in their natural need for metamorphosis?

And it seemed so strange to some that they began to doubt these young people had died at all.

"As long as we don't see two new trees," the young girl's mother said, "I will keep on hoping."

And she continued day and night, counting and recounting the trunks in the little wood, examining them one by one. No, there was no possibility of a mistake, the youngsters weren't there; in its fashion, the little wood kept impeccable records of all the region's dead. It hadn't ever been wrong.

And then one day, a week after their disappearance, two new birches were seen, one beside the other. And everybody recognized them. Perhaps the young people had wandered the neighborhood a while, before making up their minds to end their days.

But already the girl's mother was sobbing near one of the birches. And she was caressing it, no longer holding back her tears, as though *she* were here, living a new life, entirely indifferent to everything happening outside the domain of plants; no longer understanding human language, but not suffering from this lack of understanding; no longer needing affection or anything else that might touch the heart. Indeed, living the life of the trees.

NK

THE BOWL OF MILK

A worn but tenacious young man was carrying a brimming bowl of milk across Paris to his mother, who lived in a distant neighborhood and whose only source of nourishment was this milk. Every morning she watched at her window for the bowl's arrival.

The young man hurried along because he knew his mother was hungry, but he was careful not to rush so much that he spilled the liquid. Sometimes he blew on it, to nudge a little soot or a speck of dust toward the edge of the bowl, where he delicately removed it.

And occasionally the grocer at the corner of rue de Berri and rue de Penthièvre thought, *It's late—the bowl of milk went past a long time ago—and I'm not done with my display.*

"I don't want to upset you, my dear," said the young man's mother, when she saw what remained in the bowl, "but today there's less than yesterday. Poor boy, how you must have been jostled!"

"I'm going out to get another."

"Ah, you know that's impossible."

"True," said the boy, hanging his head.

It was also absolutely forbidden for him to transport the milk in a bottle. Forbidden by whom?

When the young man arrived at his mother's, his first words were always: "Drink, mama." This was his way of saying hello. He added: "Hurry up and drink. A little always evaporates." And to reassure himself that not one drop was lost, he watched the maternal Adam's apple go up and down as she swallowed.

She can't last much longer, thought the boy sadly, every day assessing the waning strength of the milk drinker.

"There's plenty in this bowl—maybe even more than I need, at my age! Besides, I feel good and strong. If I'm not well, I'll go to bed."

And it was long after she had died that her son continued to bring her milk each morning, and to rid it of soot and dust. But he kept to himself his "Drink, mama," as he went into the kitchen and emptied the bowl, with filial care, to the very last drop, into the sink.

Consider the men you pass in the street: are you sure you'd understand the reason they give for going from one part of town to another? Certainly you could question a few, and they would say, "I'm going to work" or "to the drugstore" or elsewhere. But mightn't you meet some who would be at as great a loss to answer you, if you bothered to ask, as this unfortunate boy, condemned to carry out the same gestures every day, at the same hour, come rain, come shine?

NK

Old Cemetary in Storm

LE PORTRAIT

Mère, je sais très mal comme l'on cherche les morts,
Je m'égare dans mon âme, ses visages escarpés,
Ses ronces et ses regards.
Aide-moi à revenir
De mes horizons qu'aspirent des lèvres vertigineuses,
Aide-moi à être immobile,
Tant de gestes nous séparent, tant de lévriers cruels!
Que je penche sur la source où se forme ton silence
Dans un reflet de feuillage que ton âme fait trembler.
Ah! sur ta photographie
Je ne puis pas même voir de quel côté souffle ton regard.
Nous nous en allons, pourtant, ton portrait avec moi-même,
Si condamnés l'un à l'autre
Que notre pas est semblable
Dans ce pays clandestin
Où nul ne passe que nous.
Nous montons bizarrement les côtes et les montagnes
Et jouons dans les descentes comme des blessés sans mains.
Un cierge coule chaque nuit, gicle à la face de l'aurore,
L'aurore qui tous les jours sort des draps lourds de la mort,
A demi asphyxiée,
Tardant à se reconnaître.
Je te parle durement, ma mere;
Je parle durement aux morts parce qu'il faut leur parler dur,
Debout sur des toits glissants,
Les deux mains en porte-voix et sur on ton courroucé,
Pour dominer le silence assourdissant
Qui voudrait nous séparer, nous les morts et les vivants.

J'ai de toi quelques bijoux comme des fragments de l'hiver
Qui descendent les rivières,
Ce bracelet fut de toi qui brille en la nuit d'un coffre
En cette nuit écrasée où le croissant de la lune
Tente en vain de se lever
Et recommence toujours, prisonnier de l'impossible.

THE PORTRAIT

Mother, I don't know much about looking for the dead,
I lose my way in my soul, its cliff-like faces,
Its brambles and staring eyes.
Help me to come back from my horizons
Which dizzying lips inhale,
Help me to stand still,
So many gestures come between us, so many cruel hounds!
I bend over the pool where your silence takes form
As your soul causes reflected leaves to tremble.
Ah! your photograph
Doesn't even show me the direction of your eyes, their breathing.
But we go along together, your portrait and I,
So fatefully bound to each other
We walk with the same step
Through this clandestine country
Where we are all that goes by.
Awkwardly we climb the slopes and the mountains
Playing all the way down like wounded people with no hands.
The wax a candle melts every night spurts in the face of the dawn,
The dawn emerging every day from the heavy sheets of death,
Half suffocated,
Coming only slowly to itself.
I speak to you harshly, mother,
I speak harshly to the dead -- they must be spoken to harshly,
Standing on slippery roofs,
My hands like a loud-speaker, my voice sounding angry,
To overcome the deafening silence
Which seeks to come between us, we the dead and the living.

I have a few of your jewels, like those fragments of winter
That move down rivers,
Your bracelet shines in the night of a box,
That crushed night where the crescent moon
Tries in vain to rise
Again and again, prisoner of the impossible.

J'ai été toi si fortement, moi qui le suis si faiblement,
Et si rivés tous les deux que nous eussions dû mourir ensemble
Comme deux matelots mi-noyés, s'empêchant l'un l'autre de nager,
Se donnant des coups de pied dans les profondeurs de l'Atlantique
Où commencent les poisons aveugles
Et les horizons verticaux.

Parce que tu as été moi
Je puis regarder un jardin sans penser à autre chose,
Choisir parmi mes regards,
M'en aller à ma rencontre.
Peut-être reste-t-il encore
Un ongle de tes mains parmi les ongles de mes mains,
Un de tes cils mêlé aux miens;
Un de tes battements s'égare-t-il parmi les battements de mon coeur,
Je le reconnais entre tous
Et je sais le retenir.

Mais ton coeur bat-il encore? Tu n'as plus besoin de coeur,
Tu vis séparée de toi comme si tu étais ta propre soeur,
Ma morte de vingt-huit ans,
Me regardant de trios-quarts,
Avec l'âme en équilibre et pleine de retenue.
Tu portes la même robe que rien n'usera plus,
Elle est entrée dans l'éternité avec beaucoup de douceur
Et change parfois de couleur, mais je suis seul à savoir.

Cigales de cuivre, lions de bronze, vipères d'argile,
C'est ici que rien de respire!
Le souffle de mon mensonge
Est seul à vivre alentour.
Et voici à mon poignet
Le pouls mineral des morts,
Celui-là que l'on entend si l'on approche le corps
Des strates du cimetière.

I have been you so strongly, as now I am so weakly,
So riveted to each other we should have died together
Like two half-drowned sailors who drag each other down,
Kicking at each other in the depths of the Atlantic
Where fish are blind,
Horizons vertical.

Because you were myself
I can look at a garden, not thinking of anything else,
Look where I choose to,
Go to meet myself.
Perhaps there is still
A fingernail of yours among my fingernails,
One of your eyelashes mixed in with mine
One of your heartbeats lost among my own,
I know it from all the others,
And I won't let it go.

But is your heart still beating? You don't need one any more,
You live apart from yourself as if you were your own sister,
My dead one, dead at twenty-eight,
Looking at me but somewhat turned away,
Your soul calm and decorously reserved,
Always wearing the same dress which will never
Need to be replaced,
Which entered eternity with such good grace,
If it changes color, sometimes, I'm the only one who knows.

Brass grasshoppers, bronze lions, vipers of clay,
Nothing breathes in this place,
Nothing lives,
Only the breath of my lying,
And now I feel at my wrist
The mineral pulse of the dead,
Perceptible if one brings the body close
To the stratified cemetery.

PT & KM

JULES SUPERVIELLE

THE WIDOW AND HER THREE SHEEP

A big-hearted widow had three sheep for sons. Not imitation sheep—men of little character, conformists—but the real thing, fleece and all. However, it must be said in their parents' defense that these three quadrupeds had the power of speech. What they could not do was bleat. In vain, and secretly, they tried. Impossible to make their throats issue the usual plaintive cry of wool-bearing beasts.

Neither father nor mother nor any paternal or maternal ancestors had had anything sheeplike about them. After long thought, the only plausible conjecture was that these three sheep were like those seen in Rambouillet, the town where their parents had spent their honeymoon.

They led their petit bourgeois lives as best they could. In the evening, their mother tucked each into his own bed, but the minute she turned out the light they threw off the covers and went to curl up together, all three of them, in the same corner of their bedroom.

Despite their elocutionary gifts, our sheep showed no aptitude for their studies, and not one of them managed to pass his exams, even though their mother very astutely got them recommendations from both the Society for the Prevention of Cruelty to Animals and the League for Human and Citizens' Rights. Nonetheless, the examiners refused to award diplomas to these nincompoops, freshly sheared because of the heat (exams always occurring, as everyone knows, at the beginning of summer).

Even when her husband was alive, the mother hadn't shown the least surprise at the oddness of her progeny, as though every one of her friends had given birth to sheep.

When she went out visiting, she always took along her three children, whom she called "my little lambs" in order to put everyone at ease. No simpering or affectation. No standing on their hind feet like a lapdog yapping for sugar, never any ribbons on their heads like poodles. Sheep they were, sheep they were contented to appear, which in no way hampered conversation, as people loved to hear their human voices.

"How nice of you to have brought your children!"

"I take them into society so they won't develop beastly manners."

No one was sure if you should pet them when they said, "How do you do, Madame?" and in general people settled on a friendly nod of the head.

The three behaved very properly just as long as they were given milk in saucers, since of course it would have been impossible for them to hold teacups.

The mother didn't hesitate to accept every invitation extended to her children, with the exception of garden parties, since she hadn't the heart to keep the "crazy little guys" (who disdained tea and decorum) from grazing on the lawn in front of everyone. She talked freely about their careers, their future, as if they were real little men. Should you mention to her the possibility of their marrying: "Oh, they're still young, the sweet darlings!" (What precisely was their age, in fact? Hard to tell from their ovine faces. It would have been necessary to check their teeth, but since they had the power of speech, nobody dared; they inspired a certain respect.) "They don't have jobs yet," said the mother. Or: "They're not after dowries. When the time comes, I'll find them each a serious and understanding girl who won't spend her days shopping and won't pay any attention to certain physical peculiarities that have never disgraced anyone. What does it matter, after all, if you have a nose that's too long or too short, or a little bit of wool on your back? Strength of spirit, that's what counts. Especially these days, when life is becoming so difficult."

Then, having sent them from the room for a moment, the mother added: "Would you believe that the other day a friend we have in common, I don't wish to name her, had the audacity to say to my face that it's not women but ewes these children need. The shame of it. I'll never speak to her again. If that's what's called a friend!"

Then, having summoned her children back to her side:

"My dear sons, sit down next to your mother, who is so proud of you. What little gods you are, uniting our ancestral animal experience with the intelligence and voice of humans. Believe me, there's something sacred about you…"

"Oh, mom!" they said modestly, in an excellent position to know the poverty of their tiny brains.

"It's not for you to judge. It's for your mama and your mama's true friends to say how much you're worth. I repeat that were this ancient Egypt or India you would have been *adored,* but in our mercenary time, in the absence of ideals, people are only interested in superficial appearances."

"Do you know they could make a fortune in America—" a well-intentioned friend remarked one day.

"Horrors!" said the mother. "I'd prefer my children not to go abroad. France is quite big enough for them. In a pinch I might send them to the Colonies, but to foreign countries—don't even think about it!"

The mother talked of nothing but her country: France this, France that, let's hear it for Burgundy, Picardy, Champagne, Alsace-Lorraine! French families would never make enough sacrifices, etcetera.

"And your children? What are they doing?" inquired another mother from the neighborhood, right after people had begun to die by the hundreds of thousands at Verdun.

"Don't pour salt on the wound! I'm unhappy enough as it is that I can't send my sons to the front." And with tears in her eyes, stammering with emotion: "It would be with *immamense* joy, *immamense* pride that I'd send them to fight. God has not made them for that."

When the widow took her sheep out for a walk, however, people began to give them dirty looks.

"We need meat," it was said around her. "Look at the lines in front of the butchershops."

And one day an old, decorated gentleman bowed to her very politely: "Healthy animals are beyond price. We might perhaps think about yours…"

"Murder! Sacrilege!" screamed the mother. "Don't you see my children have the power of speech!"

"Then let them pick up guns."

"Is it their fault nature only gave them four little bitty hooves that could never hold a firearm? Were this not the case, I would happily sacrifice them on the altar of the fatherland."

"We'll pick them up first thing tomorrow morning." This from the neighborhood chief of police.

Before they were slaughtered, these little woolly gentlemen were asked if they didn't wish to make a statement. It was hoped that at the moment of death they would perhaps give away the secret of their originality. But their emotion was so violent that not a word escaped their lips, and they began to bleat, to bleat as though they'd never stop, and with such misery that the executioners, in irritation, slit their throats before their turn.

NK

Sheep

JULES SUPERVIELLE

PRIÈRE À L'INCONNU

Voilà que je me surprends à t'adresser la parole,
Mon Dieu, moi qui ne sais encore si tu existes,
Et ne comprends pas la langue de tes églises chuchotantes,
Je regarde les autels, la voûte de ta maison
Comme qui dit simplement: "Voilà du bois, de la pierre,
Voilà des colonnes romanes, il manque le nez à ce saint
Et au dedans comme au dehors il y a la détresse humaine."
Je baisse les yeux sans pouvoir m'agenouiller pendant la messe
Comme si je laissais passer l'orage au-dessus de ma tête
Et je ne puis m'empêcher de penser à autre chose.
Hélas j'aurai passé ma vie à penser à autre chose,
Cette autre chose c'est encor moi, c'est peut-être mon vrai moi-même.
C'est là que je me réfugie, c'est peut-être là que tu es,
Je n'aurai jamais vécu que dans ces lointains attirants,
Le moment présent est un cadeau dont je n'ai pas su profiter,
Je ne connais pas bien l'usage, je le tourne dans tous les sens,
Sans savoir faire marcher sa mécanique difficile.
Mon Dieu, je ne crois pas en toi, je voudrais te parler tout de même;
J'ai bien parlé aux étoiles bien que je les sache sans vie,
Aux plus humbles des animaux quand je les savais sans réponse,
Aux arbres qui, sans le vent, seraient muets comme la tombe.
Je me suis parlé à moi-même quand je ne sais pas bien si j'existe.
Je ne sais si tu entends nos prières à nous les hommes,
Je ne sais si tu as envie de les écouter,
Si tu as comme nous un coeur qui est toujours sur le qui-vive,
Et des oreilles ouvertes aux nouvelles les plus différentes,
Je ne sais pas si tu aimes à regarder par ici,
Pourtant je voudrais te remettre en mémoire la planète Terre,
Avec ses fleurs, ses cailloux, ses jardins et ses maisons
Avec tous les autres et nous qui savons bien que nous souffrons.
Je veux t'adresser sans tarder ces humbles paroles humaines
Parce qu'il faut que chacun tente à présent tout l'impossible,
Même si tu n'es qu'un souffle d'il y a des milliers d'années,
Une grande vitesse acquise, une durable mélancolie

PRAYER TO THE UNKNOWN

I'm surprised to find myself speaking to you,
God, since I still don't know whether you exist,
And don't understand the whispering language of churches.
I look at your altars, the vaulting of your house,
And find nothing to say but "This is wood, this stone,
The columns are Romanesque, this saint has lost his nose,
And, inside and outside the churches, people suffer."
I lower my eyes but I can't kneel during the Mass
Which seems like a storm I allow to pass over my head
And I can't help thinking of something else,
Alas, I'll have spent my life thinking of something else,
Which does not differ from me, which may be my true self.
That's where I take refuge, perhaps that's where you are,
I'll have spent my whole life in those alluring distances;
This moment is a gift but lost on me,
I don't know what it's for, I turn it around and inside out,
But I don't know how its complex machinery works.
I don't believe in you, God — I want to talk to you anyway;
I have talked to the stars, though I know there's no life in them,
And to the humblest animals, although they could not reply,
To trees which, without the wind, would be silent as the grave —
I've talked to myself without knowing if I exist.
I don't know whether you hear our human prayers,
I don't know whether you want to hear them,
And do you have a heart like ours always on the alert,
And ears that are open to any kind of news?
I don't know whether you like to look in our direction,
But I want to remind you that there exists the planet Earth,
With its flowers, its pebbles, its gardens and its houses,
And all the others, and us, well aware of our own distress.
I'm appealing to you in this humble human speech,
Because now every one of us has to attempt the impossible,
Even if you are only a breath of air from thousands of years ago
A tremendous speed, an indestructible sadness

Qui ferait tourner encor les sphères dans leur mélodie.
Je voudrais, mon Dieu sans visage et peut-être sans espérance,
Attirer ton attention, parmi tant de ciels vagabonde,
Sur les hommes qui n'ont plus de repos sur la planète,
Écoute-moi, cela presse, ils vont tous se décourager
Et l'on ne va plus reconnaître les jeunes parmi les âgés.
Chaque matin ils se demandent si la tuerie va commencer,
De tous côtés l'on prépare de bizarres distributeurs
De sang, de plaintes et de larmes,
L'on se demande si les blés ne cachent pas déjà des fusils.
Le temps serait-il passé où tu t'occupais des hommes,
T'appelle-t-on dans d'autres mondes, médecin en consultation,
Ne sachant où donner de la tête, laissant mourir sa clientèle.
Écoute-moi, je ne suis qu'un homme parmi tant d'autres,
L'âme se plaît dans notre corps, ne demande pas à s'enfuir
Dans un éclatement de bombe,
Elle est pour nous une caresse, une secrète flatterie.
Laisse-nous respirer encor sans songer aux nouveaux poisons,
Laisse-nous regarder nos enfants sans penser tout le temps à la mort.
Nous n'avons pas du tout le coeur aux batailles, aux généraux.
Laisse-nous notre va-et-vient comme un troupeau dans ses sonnailles,
Une odeur de lait se mêlant à l'odeur de l'herbe grasse.
Ah! si tu existes, mon Dieu, regarde de notre côté,
Viens te délasser parmi nous, la Terre est belle avec ses arbres,
Ses fleuves et ses étangs, si belle que l'on dirait
Que tu la regrettes un peu.
Mon Dieu, ne va pas faire encore la sourde oreille,
Et ne va pas m'en vouloir si nous sommes à tu et à toi,
Si je te parle avec tant d'abrupte simplicité,
Je croirais moins qu'en tout autre en un Dieu qui terrorise;
Plus que par la foudre tu sais t'exprimer par les brins d'herbe,
Et par les yeux des ruisseaux et par les jeux des enfants,
Ce qui n'empêche pas les mers et les chaînes de montagnes.
Tu ne peux pas m'en vouloir de dire ce que je pense,
De réfléchir comme je peux sur l'homme et sur son existence,
Avec la franchise de la Terre et des diverses saisons
(Et peut-être de toi-même dont j'ignorais les leçons).

Still causing the spheres to turn according to their music.
God without a face, and perhaps without hope,
I want to draw your attention, among so many nomadic skies,
To humans who find no rest these days on their planet,
Listen to me, it's urgent, they will all get discouraged,
The young will look no different from the old.
Every morning they wonder if now the killing will begin,
On all sides strange devices are being prepared
To deliver blood, lamentations, tears,
Already there may be guns concealed in the wheat fields.
Do you no longer concern yourself with human beings,
Are you called to other worlds, a consulting doctor,
Solicited from all sides, letting your patients die?
Hear me, I'm only a man among so many others.
The soul enjoys our flesh, doesn't ask to be released
By the explosion of a bomb,
For us it's a caress, secretly flattering.
Let us breathe a while longer without imagining new toxins,
Let us look at our children without always thinking of death.
We have no heart at all for battles, or generals.
Let us keep moving to and fro, like a flock with its bells,
The air smelling of milk and of heavy grass.
God, if you exist, take a look in our direction,
Come and rest here — the Earth is lovely with its trees,
Its rivers and its ponds, so lovely it almost seems
That you miss it a little.
God, don't keep on turning a deaf ear to me,
Don't be offended by my informal way of speaking,
My straight-forward simplicity,
I could believe least of all in a terrifying God
Whose language is thunderbolts; yours can be blades of grass,
And the eyes of streams or the games of little children,
But also, of course, the seas and the high mountains.
You can't reproach me for speaking my mind,
For trying to understand human beings and their existence,
The Earth, and its seasons too, is out-spoken,
(And perhaps you are as well, and I didn't hear you).

Je ne suis pas sans excuses, veuille accepter mes pauvres ruses,
Tant de choses se préparent sournoisement contre nous,
Quoi que nous fassions nous craignons d'être pris au dépourvu,
Et d'être comme le taureau qui ne comprend pas ce qui se passe,
Le mène-t-on à l'abattoir, il ne sait où il va comme ça,
Et juste avant de recevoir le coup de mort sur le front
Il se répète qu'il a faim et brouterais résolument,
Mais qu'est-ce qu'ils ont ce matin avec leur tablier plein de sang
À vouloir tous s'occuper de lui?

Pontigny, juillet 1937

I have legitimate excuses, and hope you'll accept my tactics,
In the darkness so many things are preparing to attack us,
Whatever we do, we are always afraid of being unprepared,
Of being like the bull who doesn't understand what is happening,
On the way to the slaughter house
He hasn't a notion of where he is going,
And the instant before the fatal blow splits his head
He feels hungry and would gladly munch on some grass,
What's the matter with them in their bloody aprons this morning
Making such a fuss over him?

Pontigny, July 1937

PT & KM

TRISTESSE DE DIEU

(DIEU PARLE)

Je vous vois aller et venir sur le tremblement de la Terre
Comme aux premiers jours du monde, mais grande est la différence,
Mon oeuvre n'est plus en moi, je vous l'ai toute donnée.
Hommes, mes bien-aimés, je ne puis rien dans vos malheurs,
Je n'ai pu que vous donner votre courage et les larmes,
C'est la preuve chaleureuse de l'existence de Dieu.
L'humidité de votre âme c'est ce qui vous reste de moi.
Je n'ai rien pu faire d'autre.
Je ne puis rien pour la mère dont va s'éteindre le fils
Sinon vous faire allumer, chandelles de l'espérance.
S'il n'en était pas ainsi, est-ce que vous connaîtriez,
Petits lits mal défendus, la paralysie des enfants.
Je suis coupé de mon oeuvre,
Ce qui est fini est lointain et s'éloigne chaque jour.
Quand la source descend du mont comment revenir là-dessus?
Je ne sais pas plus vous parler qu'un potier ne parle à son pot,
Des deux il en est un de sourd, l'autre muet devant son oeuvre
Et je vous vois avancer vers d'aveuglants précipices
Sans pouvoir vous les nommer,
Et je ne peux vous souffler comment il faudrait s'y prendre,
Il faut vous en tirer tout seuls comme des orphelins dans la neige.
Et je me dis chaque jour au-delà d'un grand silence:
"Encore un qui fait de travers ce qu'il pourrait faire comme il faut,
Encore un qui fait un faux pas pour ne pas regarder où il doit.
Et cet autre qui se penche beaucoup trop sur son balcon
Oubliant la pesanteur,
Et celui-là qui n'a pas vérifié son moteur,
Adieu avion, adieu homme!"
Je ne puis plus rien pour vous, hélas si je me répète
C'est à force d'en souffrir.
Je suis un souvenir qui descend, vous vivez dans un souvenir,
L'espoir qui gravit vos collines, vous vivez dans une espérance.
Secoué par les prières et les blasphèmes des hommes,

GOD'S SORROW

(GOD SPEAKS)

I see you coming and going over the trembling of the Earth
The way it was in the first days, but how great is the difference now!
My creation is mine no longer, I have given it all to you.
My human beings, I love you but I cannot prevent your misfortunes,
Your courage and your tears are all I could give you,
The warm-hearted proof of God's existence.
In you there remains of me only the moisture of your soul.
That is the best I could do.
I can do nothing for the mother whose son is dying
Except cause you to light up, candles of hope.
If things were not this way, would you see,
On defenseless little beds, paralyzed children?
I am cut off from my creation,
What is finished is far away, and the distance increases.
When the stream falls down the mountainside, there's no going back.
I can't talk with you any more than a potter can talk to his pots,
One is deaf, the other stands mute before his work
And I see you moving toward vertiginous cliffs
Unable to warn you,
Unable to give you a hint about what to do,
You have to find your way alone, like orphans in the snow.
And I tell myself every day from beyond a great silence:
"Yet another one who's doing badly what he could do well,
Yet another who stumbles because he isn't looking where he's going.
And here's one who's leaning out too far on his balcony
Forgetting about gravity,
And there's one who hasn't checked his motor,
Goodbye plane, goodbye man!"
I can't do anything for you, and that makes me suffer,
That's why I repeat myself.
I am a memory descending, you live in a memory,
Hope climbs up your hills, you live in hope.
Shaken by your prayers and your blasphemies,

Je suis partout à la fois et ne peux pas me montrer,
Sans bouger je déambule et je vais de ciel en ciel,
Je suis l'errant en soi-même, et le grouillant solitaire,
Habitué des lointains, je suis très loin de moi-même,
Je m'égare au fond de moi comme un enfant dans les bois,
Je m'appelle, je me hale, je me tire vers mon centre.
Homme, si je t'ai créé c'est pour y voir un peu clair
Et pour vivre dans un corps moi qui n'ai mains ni visage.
Je veux te remercier de faire avec sérieux
Tout ce qui n'aura qu'un temps sur la Terre bien-aimée,
Ô mon enfant, mon chéri, ô courage de ton Dieu,
Mon fils qui t'en es allé courir le monde à ma place
À l'avant-garde de moi dans ton corps si vulnérable
Avec sa grande misère. Pas un petit coin de peau
Où ne puisse se former la profonde pourriture.
Chacun de vous sait faire un mort sans avoir eu besoin d'apprendre,
Un mort parfait qu'on peut tourner et retourner dans tous les sens,
Où il n'y a rien à redire.
Dieu vous survit, lui seul entouré par un grand massacre
D'hommes, de femmes et d'enfants.
Même vivants, vous mourez un peu continuellement,
Arrangez-vous avec la vie, avec vos tremblantes amours.
Vous avez un cerveau, des doigts pour faire le monde à votre goût,
Vous avez des facilités pour faire vivre la raison
Et la folie en votre cage,
Vous avez tous les animaux qui forment la Création,
Vous pouvez courir et nager comme le chien et le poisson,
Avancer comme le tigre ou comme l'agneau de huit jours,
Vous pouvez vous donner la mort comme le renne, le scorpion,
Et moi je reste l'invisible, l'introuvable sur la Terre,
Ayez pitié de votre Dieu qui n'a pas su vous rendre heureux,
Petites parcelles de moi, ô palpitantes étincelles,
Je ne vous offre qu'un brasier où vous retrouverez du feu.

I am everywhere at once and cannot show myself,
Without moving I roam from sky to sky,
I am wandering itself, solitary, abundant,
Accustomed to vast distances, I am far away from myself,
Lost in my depths like a child in the woods,
I call to myself, I haul myself in, I draw myself toward my center.
Humans, when I created you, it was to make some sense of all this,
And to inhabit a body, having no hands or face of my own.
I want to thank you for doing seriously what you do
That will last for only a while on the beloved Earth,
O my child, my darling, the courage of your God,
My son who went away to travel the world in my place,
In the forefront of me, your vulnerable body,
Its great suffering. Every bit of your skin
Susceptible to deep decay.
Not one of you needs to be taught how to make a corpse,
An impeccable corpse that can be turned over and over again,
With no fault to be found.
God survives you, he alone survives in the midst of a massacre
Of men, of women and of children.
Even while you're alive you die a little all the time,
Come to terms with life and your trembling loves.
You have a brain, your fingers can form the world as you please,
You have the means of keeping alive reason
And madness in your cage,
You have all the animals of the Creation,
You can run and swim like the dog and the fish,
You can move like the tiger or like the week-old lamb,
You can kill yourself like the reindeer or scorpion,
And I remain invisible, not to be found on Earth,
Pity your God, unable to make you happy,
Little fragments of myself, O flickering sparks,
I can offer you only a brazier where you can find fire again.

PT & KM

JULES SUPERVIELLE   141

NYMPHS

Nymphs have escaped the sky as rainwater. Forever streaming wet, they mingle their days with those of rivers and rivulets, unless they settle in the woods, where these water divinities disperse their exquisite moisture everywhere. Around them the turf turns green, and old men draw near, in the certainty of growing younger.

Daughters of the thunderheads, they are always throwing themselves into the water or being smitten with a cloud, no matter how ephemeral. They dance, they quiver only in the rain. Should drops of water fall from the sky, instantly it is the nymphs' season for love. The sun would dry their hearts up, if they did not flee from it in all their wild whiteness. Their eyes are blue, the only concession they make to good weather. But their tears, strangers to salt, are sweet and fresh as rain.

Not all nymphs descend from the heavens. In certain places, generally at the base of trees, it happens that the blades of grass grow finer and closer together, water there mirrors the azure with more brilliance and more tenderness, and even the air alights more gingerly. From faraway come satyrs and aegipans, veritable dowsers of forest divinities, to sniff out the place: a nymph is brewing here. And in fact if you look carefully, you see beneath some puddle, mingling with the earth but never soiled by it, an adorable arm or shoulder. Only later does the head appear, when the whole body is ready to receive it. And just barely complete, the nymph stands up and looks around her, as if seeking a companion. The latter presents herself immediately and comes forward with smiles of welcome to whisper in her new friend's ear.

Nymphs are born already willowy and sensitive to love. Such beauty and grace have never passed through childhood, yet retain its glint and dazzling freshness.

Have trees anything to do with the arrival in this world of the nymphs born at their feet? They like to think so, and it hurts us to enlighten them. But it must be recognized that the fathers of these divinities are un-known—perhaps even multiple—since nymphs arise simultaneously from earth, sky and water. Which protects them against familial worries. A father, whether he be river, cloud or tree, is not too inconvenient. His reproaches remain obscure, and it's easy to escape them by seeking other waters, other skies, other shady canopies.

The nymphs' only lovers are satyrs, aegipans and fauns, all very violent, very impatient and, once the pleasures of lovemaking are over, as neglectful as roosters are of hens.

But there is a secret nymph among all the others, the hamadryad. She does not leave the tree that gave birth to her. She is the hidden fruit of its fiber. In the freshness of its sap she finds what men call home. The tree responds to the nymph's tenderness with mute consideration. But is the silence of a tree entirely trustworthy? Just when you were least expecting it, a little breeze, a puff of wind, and there's the tree starting to speak confusedly. Whirlwinds of words escape it, though they do not form a sentence.

"What's that you're saying?" asks the hamadryad, with perfect courtesy.

And the tree emits more sounds, every bit as impenetrable. The nymph doesn't exist.

Being of completely different proportions and consistencies, the tree and its hamadryad can only love each other chastely. They are meant for each other nonetheless, in that one encloses the other; they marry one another's form. But there the relationship ends. This is a love almost as pure as the poet's for the stars or the child's for his kite in the instant when it flies the highest. Much more than a lover, the tree is the very clothing and jewels of the hamadryad. No matter where she goes in the trunk or branches, she always finds a way to make space for herself: yes, as elastic as a divinity...

Certain hamadryads lack the courage to die at the same time as their felled trees. They take refuge in some neighboring trunk, lightning-struck and deserted by its companion. There, they form a group of sickly widows, gazing around them as though expecting the arrival and pity of some improbable painter, come to illustrate their anguish.

The hamadryads use any and all means to keep the woodcutter from chopping down their tree. As soon as he appears, they all inveigh against him: "What are you planning to do with my tree? It's scarcely even oak, it's really *oakum*. Just look around you. You'll see many more solid trunks. Out of them you can make fires, furniture, happiness of every kind!"

The eloquence of certain hamadryads is such that they enable a few trees to become centenarians—even to reach a thousand years. But whatever the trees' age may be, their lovely guardians stay no less young: they are all thirteen to eighteen, no more, no less.

NK

LA GOUTTE DE PLUIE

(DIEU PARLE)

Je cherche une goutte de pluie
Qui vient de tomber dans la mer.
Dans sa rapide verticale
Elle luisait plus que les autres
Car seule entre les autres gouttes
Elle eut la force de comprendre
Que, très douce dans l'eau salée,
Elle allait se perdre à jamais.
Alors je cherche dans la mer
Et sur les vagues, alertées,
Je cherche pour faire plaisir
À ce fragile souvenir
Dont je suis seul dépositaire.
Mais j'ai beau faire, il est des choses
Où Dieu même ne peut plus rien.
Malgré sa bonne volonté
Et l'assistance sans paroles
Du ciel, des vagues et de l'air.

RAINDROP

(GOD SPEAKS)

I am looking for a raindrop
That has just fallen into the sea.
Gleaming the length of its plummet
More than any of the others,
This raindrop alone among them
Had the power to understand
That very sweet in salt water
It would soon be lost forever.
And so I look in the sea
And on the now vigilant waves
Trying at least to do something
For that fragile memory
Which entrusted itself to my care.
But it's no use; there are things
Which cannot be helped
Even by God, despite His good will
And the wordless intervention
Of the sky, the waves, and the air.

PT & KM

SUPERVIELLE TEXTS INCLUDED IN THIS VOLUME
IN ORDER OF THEIR PUBLICATION

"La Estancia"/"The Estancia" : *Uruguay,* 1928

"Gauchos"/"Gauchos" : *Uruguay,* 1928

"Dans la forêt sans heures"/"No Hours in the Forest" : *Le Forçat innocent,* 1930

"L'Enfant de la haute mer"/"Child of the High Seas" : *L'Enfant de la haute mer,* 1931

"Le Boeuf et l'âne de la crèche/"The Ox and the Donkey in the Manger" : *L'Enfant de la haute mer,* 1931

"L'Inconnue de la Seine"/"The Unknown Girl of the Seine" : *L'Enfant de la haute mer,* 1931

"La Piste et la mare"/"The Trail and the Pond" : *L'Enfant de la haute mer,* 1931

"Le Portrait"/"The Portrait" : *Gravitations,* 1932

"47 Boulevard Lannes"/"47 Boulevard Lannes" : *Gravitations,* 1932

"Le Survivant"/"The Survivor" : *Gravitations,* 1932

"Pointe de flamme"/"Flame Tip" : *Gravitations,* 1932

"A Lautréamont"/"To Lautréamont" : *Gravitations,* 1932

"Le Regret de la Terre"/"Missing the Earth" : *Les Amis inconnus,* 1934

"Le Sillage"/"Wake" : *Les Amis inconnus,* 1934

"Un poète"/"A Poet" : *Les Amis inconnus,* 1934

"La Demeure entourée"/"The House Surrounded" : *Les Amis inconnus,* 1934

"L'Arche de Noé"/"Noah's Ark" : *L'Arche de Noé,* 1938

"La Fuite en Égypte"/"The Flight into Egypt" : *L'Arche de Noé,* 1938

"Le Bol de lait"/"The Bowl of Milk" : *L'Arche de Noé,* 1938

"Dieu parle à l'homme"/"God Talks to Man" : *La Fable du monde,* 1938

"La Goutte de pluie"/"Raindrop" : *La Fable du monde,* 1938

"Prière à l'inconnu"/"Prayer to the Unknown" : *La Fable du monde,* 1938

"Tristesse de Dieu"/"God's Sorrow" : *La Fable du monde,* 1938

"Tu disparais"/"You Disappear" : *1939–1945,* 1946

"Genèse"/"Genesis" : *Oublieuse mémoire,* 1949

"Les Nymphes"/"Nymphs" : *Premiers pas de l'univers,* 1950

"Le Petit Bois"/"The Little Wood" : *Premiers pas de l'univers,* 1950

"La Veuve aux trois moutons"/"The Widow and Her Three Sheep" : *Premiers pas de l'univers,* 1950

"La Sanglante Métamorphose"/"Metamorphosis in Blood" : *L'Escalier,* 1956

Débarcadères. Editions de la Revue de l'Amérique latine, 1922. Poems.

L'Homme de la pampa. N.R.F., 1923. Novel.

Le Voleur d'enfants. Gallimard, 1926. Novel.

Oloron-Sainte-Marie. Cahiers du Sud, 1927. Poems.

Le Survivant. N.R.F., 1928. Novel.

Uruguay. Emile-Paul frères, 1928. Memoir.

Le Forçat innocent. Gallimard, 1930. Poems.

L'Enfant de la haute mer. Gallimard, 1931. Tales.

Gravitations: Edition définitive. Gallimard, 1932. [Earlier edition: Gallimard, 1925.] Poems.

Les Amis inconnus. Gallimard, 1934. Poems.

L'Arche de Noé. Gallimard, 1938. Tales.

La Fable du monde. Gallimard, 1938. Poems.

Le Petit Bois et autres contes. Mexico: Editions Quetzel, 1942. Tales.

1939−1945. Gallimard, 1946. Poems.

Oublieuse mémoire. Gallimard, 1949. Poems.

Premiers pas de l'univers. Gallimard, 1950. Tales.

Boire à la source, Confidences, nouvelle édition augmentée. Gallimard, 1951. [Earlier edition: Corrêa, 1933.] Memoir.

L'Escalier. Gallimard, 1956. Poems.

ENGLISH TRANSLATIONS OF JULES SUPERVIELLE

Selected Writings of Jules Supervielle. Trans. James Kirkup, Denise Levertov, Enid McLeod, Alan Pryce-Jones, Kenneth Rexroth. New Directions, 1967.

Jules Supervielle: Selected Poems and Reflections on the Art of Poetry. Trans. George Bogin. SUN, 1985.

Homesick for the Earth: Selected Poems of Jules Supervielle, with versions by Moniza Alvi. Bloodaxe, 2012.

THE TRANSLATORS

NANCY KLINE's translations, short stories, memoirs, essays, and reviews have appeared widely. She has been awarded a National Endowment for the Arts Creative Writing Grant and has published seven books: a novel (*The Faithful*); a critical study of the poetry of René Char (*Lightning*); a biography of Elizabeth Blackwell M.D. (*A Doctor's Triumph*); an annotated translation of Claudine Herrmann's *Les Voleuses de langue (The Tongue Snatchers);* a collection of essays on the teaching of writing (*How Writers Teach Writing,* as editor and contributor); and new translations of Paul Eluard's *Capital of Pain* (with Mary Ann Caws and Patricia Terry) and René Char's *Furor and Mystery and Other Writings* (with Mary Ann Caws). From 1989 to 2007 she taught in the English and French departments at Barnard College, where she was founding director of the Writing Fellows Program. She has also taught at Harvard, UCLA, the University of Massachusetts Boston, and Wellesley, and under the auspices of Poets & Writers and the Bard Prison Initiative. She is currently an Associate at the Bard Institute for Writing & Thinking. As a French major at Barnard, many years ago, she studied translation under Patricia Terry, who became a dear friend and a crucial colleague. Pat was among *the precious few.*

PATRICIA TERRY was Professor of French Literature at Barnard College and subsequently at the University of California San Diego until her retirement in 1991. Among her verse translations are *Poems of Jules Laforgue, The Song of Roland, Poems of the Elder Edda, The Honeysuckle and the Hazel Tree, Renard the Fox,* and *Roof Slates and Other Poems of Pierre Reverdy* (with Mary Ann Caws). Recent titles include *Capital of Pain* by Paul Eluard (with Mary Ann Caws and Nancy Kline), an illustrated edition of *Lancelot and the Lord of the Distant Isles: Or, the Book of Galehaut Retold* (with Samuel N. Rosenberg), *The Sea and Other Poems* by Guillevic, *Essential Poems & Prose of Jules Laforgue,* and a book of her own poetry, *Words of Silence.*

KATHLEEN MICKLOW lived in various regions of France between 1959 and 1963. She later taught French literature at Barnard College and at the Riverdale Country School, where she was Head of the Foreign Language Department. From 1965 on, when she and Pat Terry were colleagues at Barnard, they collaborated on translations of poets as diverse as Villon, Laforgue, Eluard and Guillevic. They also shared such other interests as Tai Chi, Buddhist practice, medieval literature, travel in France, and Pat's own poetry.

BLACK WIDOW PRESS

TRANSLATION SERIES

A Life of Poems, Poems of a Life
by Anna de Noailles.
Translation: Norman R. Shapiro.
Introduction: Catherine Perry.

Approximate Man and Other Writings
by Tristan Tzara. Translation: Mary Ann Caws.

Art Poétique by Guillevic.
Translation: Maureen Smith.

The Big Game by Benjamin Péret.
Translation/introduction: Marilyn Kallet.

Capital of Pain by Paul Eluard.
Translation: Mary Ann Caws, Patricia Terry,
and Nancy Kline.

Chanson Dada: Selected Poems by Tristan Tzara.
Translation/introduction/essay: Lee Harwood.

Essential Poems and Writings of Joyce Mansour:
A Bilingual Anthology
Translation/introduction: Serge Gavronsky.

Essential Poems and Prose of Jules Laforgue
Translated and edited: Patricia Terry.

Essential Poems and Writings of Robert Desnos:
A Bilingual Anthology
Edited/introduction/essay: Mary Ann Caws.

EyeSeas (Les Ziaux) by Raymond Queneau.
Translation/introduction: Daniela Hurezanu
and Stephen Kessler.

Furor and Mystery & Other Writings
by René Char. Edited and translated:
Mary Ann Caws and Nancy Kline.

Guarding the Air:
Selected Poems of Gunnar Harding
Translated and edited: Roger Greenwald.

The Inventor of Love & Other Writings
by Gherasim Luca. Translation: Julian & Laura
Semilian. Introduction: Andrei Codrescu.
Essay: Petre Răileanu.

La Fontaine's Bawdy by Jean de La Fontaine.
Translation/introduction:
Norman R. Shapiro.

Last Love Poems of Paul Eluard
Translation/introduction: Marilyn Kallet.

Love, Poetry (L'amour la poésie) by Paul Eluard.
Translation/essay: Stuart Kendall.

Poems of André Breton: A Bilingual Anthology
Translation/essays: Jean-Pierre Cauvin and
Mary Ann Caws.

Poems of A. O. Barnabooth by Valéry Larbaud.
Translation: Ron Padgett and Bill Zavatsky.

Poems of Consummation by Vicente Aleixandre.
Translation: Stephen Kessler

Préversities: A Jacques Prévert Sampler
Translation/edited: Norman R. Shapiro.

The Sea and Other Poems by Guillevic.
Translation: Patricia Terry. Introduction:
Monique Chefdor.

Selected Prose and Poetry of Jules Supervielle
Edited, with an Introduction: Nancy Kline.
Translation: Nancy Kline, Patricia Terry, and
Kathleen Micklow.

To Speak, to Tell You? Poems by Sabine Sicaud.
Translation: Norman R. Shapiro.
Introduction and notes: Odile Ayral-Clause.

forthcoming translations

Boris Vian Invents Boris Vian:
A Boris Vian Reader
Edited and translated: Julia Older.

Earthlight (Claire de Terre) by André Breton.
Translation: Bill Zavatsky and Zack Rogrow
(new and revised edition).

Fables for the Modern Age by Pierre Coran.
Edited and translated: Norman R. Shapiro.
Illustration: Olga Pastuchiv.

Pierre Reverdy: Poems Early to Late
Translation: Mary Ann Caws and
Patricia Terry.

MODERN POETRY SERIES

WWW.BLACKWIDOWPRESS.COM